Collaborative Research in Multilingual Classrooms

CRITICAL LANGUAGE AND LITERACY STUDIES
Series Editors: Professor Vaidehi Ramanathan, *University of California, USA,*
Professor Bonny Norton, *University of British Columbia, Canada,*
Professor Alastair Pennycook, *University of Technology, Sydney, Australia*

Critical Language and Literacy Studies is an international series that encourages
monographs directly addressing issues of power (its flows, inequities, distributions,
trajectories) in a variety of language- and literacy-related realms. The aim with
this series is twofold: (1) to cultivate scholarship that openly engages with social,
political and historical dimensions in language and literacy studies, and (2) to widen
disciplinary horizons by encouraging new work on topics that have received little
focus (see below for partial list of subject areas) and that use innovative theoretical
frameworks.

Full details of all the books in this series and of all our other publications can be
found on http://www.multilingual-matters.com, or by writing to Multilingual
Matters, St Nicholas House, 31–34 High Street, Bristol BS1 2AW, UK.

CRITICAL LANGUAGE AND LITERACY STUDIES
Series Editors: Professor Vaidehi Ramanathan, Professor Bonny Norton,
Professor Alastair Pennycook

Collaborative Research in Multilingual Classrooms

Corey Denos, Kelleen Toohey,
Kathy Neilson and Bonnie Waterstone

With Linda Hof, Roumiana Ilieva,
Suzanne Rowbotham, Sonia Sandhu,
Susie Sandhu, Anne Scholefield,
Joanne Thompson, Colleen Tsoukalas

MULTILINGUAL MATTERS
Bristol • Buffalo • Toronto

Library of Congress Cataloging in Publication Data
A catalog record for this book is available from the Library of Congress.
Collaborative Research in Multilingual Classrooms
Corey Denos et al.
Critical Language and Literacy Studies: 1
Includes bibliographical references.
1. Language and education. I. Denos, Corey Hawes
P40.8.C64 2009
370.117'50973–dc22 2008035202

British Library Cataloguing in Publication Data
A catalogue entry for this book is available from the British Library.

ISBN-13: 978-1-84769-137-8 (hbk)
ISBN-13: 978-1-84769-136-1 (pbk)

Multilingual Matters
UK: St Nicholas House, 31–34 High Street, Bristol BS1 2AW, UK.
USA: UTP, 2250 Military Road, Tonawanda, NY 14150, USA.
Canada: UTP, 5201 Dufferin Street, North York, Ontario M3H 5T8, Canada.

The policy of Multilingual Matters/Channel View Publications is to use papers
that are natural, renewable and recyclable products, made from wood grown in
sustainable forests. In the manufacturing process of our books, and to further
support our policy, preference is given to printers that have FSC and PEFC Chain
of Custody certification.TheFSCand/orPEFClogoswillappearonthosebooks
where full certificationhasbeengrantedtotheprinterconcerned.

Typeset by Techset Composition Ltd., Salisbury, UK.

Dedication

Corey Denos

I want to dedicate this book first to the hundreds of children and their families who so graciously and generously allowed me to travel with them along their ways. Their gifts have broadened and enriched my appreciation of our world and given me confidence in our future. I am deeply grateful, as well, to the many wonderful teachers whose work has guided and supported me throughout my life.

Kelleen Toohey

I would like to dedicate this book to all its co-authors and other members of TARG (including Chris Stewart and Satnam Chohal). I have seldom had such rich collegial conversation as I have experienced in this group. Working over many years with such wise and thoughtful colleagues has affected my teaching and thinking profoundly. I owe them all an immense debt for their commitment to trying to be hopeful about public education.

Kathy Neilson

With thanks to TARG, whose gritty, astute, unreserved and immediate caring has touched so many lives, including mine.

Bonnie Waterstone

I would like to dedicate this book to all the members of TARG over the years, whose commitment to engaging in the critical conversations necessary to create more just and loving conditions in schools has inspired me and influenced my own work. I am particularly grateful to those who gathered around the oval table in those first years, when the strong roots were nurtured for the development of this remarkable group.

Contents

Preface

Although action research has come of age in second language scholarship, its connections to power, inequities and identities are recent, and the present volume highlights various aspects of these issues in a remarkable way. Grounded in the daily lives of diverse classroom communities, while drawing on a wide range of innovative theory, *Collaborative Research in Multilingual Classrooms* by Corey Denos, Kelleen Toohey, Kathy Neilson and Bonnie Waterstone, with its diverse contributions from eight additional participants, is particularly well suited to our series 'Critical Language and Literacy Studies'. Centrally concerned with the promotion of inclusive teaching, educational change and social justice, the authors, who refer to themselves as the Teacher Action Research Group (TARG), document their five-year collaborative research in multilingual elementary classrooms, with a view to investigating how classroom inequities can be better understood and creatively addressed. Central questions for the group include, 'Who "belongs" in classrooms? Who has power in classrooms?' and focal students are English language learners and students with special needs.

The purpose of the book, however, is not to develop a set of 'how to' instructions for teachers, but to provide a forum in which insights can be shared, challenges discussed and possibilities explored. Classroom vignettes and narrative observations are highlighted throughout the text, inspired by the words of the children's novelist, Philip Pullman, who wrote: '"Thou shalt not" might reach the head, but it takes "Once upon a time" to reach the heart'. Thus what distinguishes this work from much action research in the educational community is the innovative way in which it weaves together the experiences of diverse stakeholders, from teachers, students and scholars, to parents and community members. The highly accomplished teachers Corey Denos and Kathy Neilson have played a significant role in making sense of this exciting collaboration, while Bonnie Waterstone, in her role as doctoral candidate, has been well-placed to offer insightful observations of the unfolding narratives (see also Toohey & Waterstone, 2004; Waterstone, 2003).

Other characteristics of this book are also very appealing to a series on critical language and literacy studies, three of which are particularly noteworthy. The first concerns the genesis and composition of the research team itself; the second addresses the unit of analysis used throughout the book, that is, the classroom practices that have served to either constrain or enable the learning opportunities of students; and the third has to do with the focus on the multilingual resources that students bring to their classes in the context of enhanced relations between schools, homes and communities.

What then, were the primary characteristics of TARG, that evolved over the years from a research group into what they have called a 'learning community'? When TARG was first constituted by Kelleen Toohey in 1999, it sought to determine what insights, resources and practices, arising from classroom research, might be most helpful for teachers in multilingual, multicultural classrooms. Toohey's then recently published book (Toohey, 2000), had been aimed primarily at an academic audience, and TARG provided the opportunity to shift this audience to teachers in classrooms. Over time, as the group cohered and developed an identity in its own right, TARG saw itself as a learning community, and began to consider ways in which the vibrancy of this adult learning community might be recreated for learners and students. As Suzanne Rowbotham put it, 'People learn best when they are taking active and varying roles in their working community'.

Clearly, all members of TARG were highly committed to a common project, that is, to better understand those students who struggled to learn within their classrooms, and to creatively consider how to transform their learning experience. Although the group shared a common purpose, however, it is significant that the members of the group were highly diverse, spanning a wide range of age and experience, and speaking a variety of languages, including Punjabi, Bulgarian, French, Japanese and English. Whereas most members of the group were experienced elementary school teachers, there were also graduate students, as well as a video ethnographer. Each member of the group thus brought unique perspectives to the discussion, and there was much mutual respect for one another's contributions. As the authors note, 'Experiencing how our various expertises are of use to the group, with no one of us having responsibility for being always a knower or always a learner, has been one of our many pleasures'. Further, because the group included diverse stakeholders, there was much opportunity to incorporate into the analysis a wide variety of source material, including classroom narratives, teacher reflections and published scholarship. In addition, the fact that the group met on a regular basis, over many years, allowed participants to consider not only how students change over time, but how TARG participants themselves could change, grow and adapt to diverse circumstances.

There are two important aspects to this tradition of critical action research. First, it draws on the work of authors such as Carr and Kemmis, and their focus on reflective practice and social change. This framing of research has always connected action to praxis 'that continuous reflexive integration of thought, desire and action' (Simon, 1992: 49), and has always been concerned not only with reflection and classroom change but also with the broader social and political contexts of such change. Second, it links to those researchers who have managed that difficult task of carrying on collaborative work across the academy/school divide (a two-way street in which not only academics need to make their research relevant in school settings, but teachers have to be able to articulate the implications of their practice). This team's research can be seen in the tradition established by researchers such as Elsa Auerbach, whose approach to 'participatory action research' has always had a focus on questions of power and inequality, on community exploration of issues of concern to them and on the collaborative production of research out-comes. Who sets the research agenda? Who is involved in gathering data? Whose interests to the outcomes serve? Who benefits from the research? (Auerbach, 1994: 694). Whereas Auerbach's work drew on Freirean peda-gogy and was oriented particularly towards adult ESL, this book focuses on much younger students and draws on a variety of sources from Freire and Luke, to Lather and Walkerdine.

Whilst the narratives of teachers and students are woven throughout the text, exploring themes of identity, community, helping and possibility, what serves as the unit of analysis is the classroom practices that promote learning, particularly for English language learners. This is a crucial point that researchers such as Rampton (1995) underscore. Classroom practices can be seen to mediate between language inheritances and language allegiances (Miller, 2004) and as Leung *et al.* (1997) point out, the space of classroom practices is particularly relevant to the competencies of migrant students, whose language expertise, affiliation and inheritance in the first language is likely to undergo all kinds of shifts in their acquiring of second and third languages. It is the space through which the socially situated identities of speakers is at once highlighted and extended (Hawkins, 2004; Norton, 2000). As Kelleen Toohey notes in one reflection, 'For me, the important thing is, don't focus on diagnosing or fixing the kid (or even the teacher) and instead focus on the practices'. By focusing on the practices, Suzanne Rowbotham notes, teachers can avoid practices that 'force students into defensive positions, and... actively challenge and resist the equation of *difference* with *problem*'. TARG members debated, for example, how certain practices such as those associated with evaluation, differentially position both teachers and students, frequently compromising attempts to create more powerful identities for learners. Such practices are illustrative of the integral relationship between local educational activities, on the one hand, and broader national agendas, on the other. This focus on practices and activities, theoretically motivated by the work of scholars such as Vygotsky, Lave and Wenger, and Rogoff, is particularly helpful in educational settings, as it allows for extrapolation to other contexts, and readers are invited to reflect on TARG's discussions on classroom practices in the context of their own time and place.

Teachers were not only concerned with isolated 'strategies', however, but with more fundamental questions about the distribution of power and resources within classrooms, and the ways in which certain practices constrain or enable the construction of more powerful identities for learners. The buddy system, for example, expertly captured on video by Linda Hof, and insightfully reviewed by Joanne Thomson, comes under careful scrutiny. Thompson learnt that designating one learner as 'helper' and the other as 'less knowledgeable' can have negative and unintended consequences, not only for the students, but for the rest of the class. The narratives of students such as Raminder, Surjeet, Jennifer, Tim, Ashif and Jake, likewise, raise important questions about the way students are positioned by other students, their teachers, families and the wider community. Although these learners were frequently essentialised as poor learners, with negative attitudes and behaviours, careful observation, frequently with the assistance of video ethnography, highlighted more complex identities, with ongoing struggles for recognition and respect. In this view, a 'poor' learner – or a 'good' learner – is one who has frequently been constructed as such by the practices of the classroom and community (see also Norton & Toohey, 2001).

It is important to note further that teachers, too, are not immune to struggles over power and identity. As Sonia Sandhu notes, 'I worried about the noise level – would my colleagues think that I didn't have good classroom management?' Sonia Sandhu had to learn how to 'breathe' in order to allow for flexibility and adaptability in her classrooms, and argues convincingly that both teachers and students need to feel safe if effective learning is to take place. Anne Scholefield uses the metaphor of 'balancing rocks' to make a similar case, arguing that once the teacher has helped create the conditions for learning, she should give the students space to negotiate their own experiences. Such learning, Susie Sandhu notes, is enhanced with more effective home-school connections, and she provides multiple opportunities for parents and grandparents to integrate themselves into the life of her classroom. Families, she argues, 'are the children's first teachers, and as an educator I need to learn more from them'. This comment points to the third salient feature of this book: its focus on multilingualism as a resource, in the context of enhanced relationships between schools, homes and communities. The authors and researchers of this book take a view of schools as deeply interlinked with families, communities and the wider social context in which schooling happens. Not only does this allow for broader collaboration across the community and the possibility of a wider integration of home-school relations, but it also makes possible the conception of student resources as positive and productive. Community multilingualism is almost never seen as a problem: people get on with their multilingual lives, drawing on their varied linguistic resources according to the different contexts they encounter. It is only when community multilingualism comes into educational contexts that it starts to be a problem. The challenge for teachers is to work out how to draw on the multilingual and multicultural capacities the students bring to class, not in terms of lip-service to festivals and cultural icons, but rather in terms of community practices. This book gives us some important insights into how this can be done.

Collaborative Research in Multilingual Classrooms invites readers into exciting, noisy, creative classrooms in which multilingualism is valued and difference respected. Without neglecting the complex challenges teachers face, the authors document with insight and flair how the resources that diverse students bring to school can be integrated into the very fabric of classroom life, creating innovative spaces for learning and educational change. In doing so, TARG has generously extended its learning community to embrace a wide range of teachers, students and researchers in the international community. As series editors, we are delighted that the first book in this new series has brought together these important themes so successfully.

References

Auerbach, E. (1994) Participatory action research. *TESOL Quarterly* 28 (4), 693–697.
Carr, W. and Kemmis, S. (1986) *Becoming Critical: Education, Knowledge and Action Research*. Lewes: Falmer.
Denos, C. (2003) Negotiating for positions of power in a primary classroom. *Language Arts* 80, 6.
Hawkins, M. (2004) Social apprenticeships through mediated learning in language teacher education. In M. Hawkins (ed.) *Language Learning and Teacher Education* (pp. 89–109). Clevedon: Multilingual Matters.

Leung, C., Harris, R. and Rampton, B. (1997) The idealized native speaker, reified ethnicities and classroom realities. *TESOL Quarterly* 31, 543–560.

Miller, J. (2004) Social languages and schooling: The uptake of sociocultural perspectives in school. In M. Hawkins (ed.) *Language Learning and Teacher Education* (pp. 113–146). Clevedon: Multilingual Matters.

Norton, B. (2000) *Identity and Language Learning: Gender, Ethnicity and Educational Change.* Harlow: Longman/Pearson Education.

Norton, B. and Toohey, K. (2001) Changing perspectives on good language learners. *TESOL Quarterly* 35 (2), 307–322.

Rampton, B. (1995) *Crossing: Language and Ethnicity among Adolescents.* London: Longman.

Simon, R. (1992) *Teaching Against the Grain: Essays Towards a Pedagogy of Possibility.* Boston: Bergin & Garvey.

Toohey, K. (2000) *Learning English at School: Identity, Social Relations and Classroom Practice.* Clevedon: Multilingual Matters.

Toohey, K. and Waterstone, B. (2004) Negotiating expertise in an action research community. In B. Norton and K. Toohey (eds) *Critical Pedagogies and Language Learning.* New York: Cambridge University Press.

Waterstone, B. (2003) Self, genre, community: Negotiating the landscape of a teacher/researcher collaboration. Unpublished doctoral dissertation, Simon Fraser University.

Bonny Norton, Alastair Pennycook, and Vaidehi Ramanathan
September 2008

Chapter 1
Introduction

The Little Girl Who Wanted a Hug

Corey Denos

She is tall for her years, with the long dark, gently curling hair and eyelashes I yearned for when I was her age. Her family is from Iraq, which she refers to as 'my country', and consists of her father, mother and three younger brothers. For the first several weeks at school beginning in September, she was just one of 24 new faces and names. Her name was hard for me to pronounce correctly. Her quiet nature made it difficult for me to determine how well she understood English and, at the same time, easy for me take care of the needs of other, more boisterous and disruptive students first. She became a special person to me one October morning when she brought a drawing to me. It had been done in pencil and showed five pairs of long figures facing each other. In each pair, one figure was shorter than the other and was apparently offering something to the taller one – a box tied with a bow, a small bunch of flowers, a heart ... 'Oh my!' I said. 'Please tell me about your picture.' 'It's about a little girl who wants a hug', she said quietly.

Since then she comes to talk to me almost every day. She is very polite, waiting until other children have finished telling me ... what happened to them last night, that they forgot to bring their lunch, could they go to the library to get a new book, who budged on the way into the building ... and then checking, 'I have something to tell you about. Is it okay if I tell you? ... Now? ... Is it okay now?' And then she tells me ...

> *You know what my mom does? She puts an egg in milk and makes me drink it and I do not want to. She says it's good. Is that true? Would you do that? If you say it's good then I like it. ... But why doesn't anyone else*

Continued

1

eat it? I don't see anyone else ... so I think it's wrong. When you put the egg in, it makes the milk yellow.

You know my mother doesn't speak English?

Well, when my mother talks on the phone she says 'I'll kill you'. It sort of scares me. But then I know she means 'I'll call you'. So I teach her, 'Say call not kill'. I teach her to say 'I'll call you'. Not 'I'll kill you'.

My mom wears a scarf. What do you think? (I think your mom is very pretty.) Oh. (Will you wear a scarf when you are older?) Yes.

I am teaching my little brother – letters and numbers and plusses and take aways. His teacher says he's lazy because he can't do anything. My dad tried to teach him but he still doesn't know anything. So I'm teaching him. If I teach him forever, he'll be the smartest boy in the world. So I guess I'll have to teach him forever.

When my mom and dad go to work I have to babysit. One time my baby brother woke up and he wanted my mom. And he cried. And I cried too because I tried everything. Then finally I put him on my back and he stopped.

When I'm babysitting we play school and I teach my brothers. My dad teaches letters and stuff, but I teach very important things. I teach how to behave so my dad won't get mad. I tell them that when my dad calls them to come, they should come. Sometimes they won't come when my dad wants ... and my mom too. But they come if I call. And they shouldn't hit and fight either. That's what I teach. What do you think?

(January 27) Did we have Christmas? Is it over? When was it? I saw Santa Claus. My uncle and me and my brothers saw him. We sat on his lap and he said what do you want for Christmas? I said a Barbie doll and my brothers said guns. You know, not real ones. Santa Claus said he would bring them but he didn't. Why didn't he come? (I don't know how to answer that question.) I think I can. I think he didn't know where my house is. What do you think? He should have asked where I lived.

I wish Jovan and Nathalie and Jasmine would like me. (But they don't?) No. (Why do you think?) Because I'm not the best? ... But Irma likes me.

Continued

Would you do something for me? I brought these little toys and I want you to give them to the other kids. I think when you give things to other people it makes them happy. What do you think?

There's something you said that came true. Yesterday you said that tomorrow Irma and Paige would be my friends again ... and it's true! They are! How did you do that?

And so go our conversations ... as she daily gifts me with pieces from her life. It is clear that she thinks hard about what she's going to say ahead of time, and sometimes I have to struggle to figure out what she's really asking. But it seems to me that somewhere in almost every one of her conversations lies the basic question, 'Am I okay? I can see that I am different, but is where I belong and what I am, okay? What do you think?'

She is eight years old. According to provincially-given 'standards' she is 'not yet meeting expectations' in reading and writing and mathematics. She is seen by the Learning Assistance teacher and the ESL teacher, both of whom complain repeatedly – first, that she smells bad – and second, that she's not making any progress. In December she was given tests that showed she has Moderate Intellectual Disability. She has been waiting for resource room placement ever since. Several years ago her family became involved with social workers at Family Services who felt that the parents needed support in parenting and health issues. The two of her younger brothers who have started school have already had problems with aggressive behavior. Her father has had repeated problems with the police.

Two years have passed. Last year the family announced it was moving to Afghanistan and, within days, disappeared.

But she is still with me. I find the complexities of her situation painful to consider and beyond untangling. In the middle, however, is the clear beauty of the little girl – her burning desire to know herself, to make sense of the world, and to make whatever it is better. I am truly blessed to have known her. I look for her now in all of my students – and give them a hug.

While the difficulties faced by The Little Girl Who Wanted a Hug are overwhelming – learning English as a second language (ESL), an intellectual disability, an abusive father, poverty and more – she, along with Jake and Raminder and Surjeet and the others whose stories are told in this book, can be seen as representative of all students in all classrooms. She, like all children, is struggling to figure out who she is and to decide whether that is okay. She is struggling to become an active participant in her classroom community. She brings resources to her struggle; she knows she is a good babysitter and teacher of her younger brothers and sisters. She knows she is learning English well and she corrects her mom's English pronunciation. However, she is somewhat puzzled by school in this new country and she looks to her teacher for support – for some of the information she needs to negotiate a place for herself in this new setting. This particular little girl may be unusually articulate and uncommonly forthright in her insistence on help from her teacher. But the big questions she asks are the questions we all must answer. And her teacher, like most teachers, knows that the answers matter.

It is a HARD job, being a teacher. For one thing, we do not have very much time to do the job we set for ourselves. In Canada, children enter our lives in September and are gone in June. They arrive already highly complex individuals – as big as life, in the middle of their own stories and then they go away – for better or worse, with no endings, happy or otherwise. Most of the time we do not have the opportunity to learn what happened next or to reflect on the effects of whatever decisions we made in our attempts to help with those big questions.

As well, today's classrooms are fabulously diverse, and teachers are both privileged and challenged to be sharing their days with children who come from experiences virtually incomprehensible to them – children intimately familiar with poverty, war and violence … living with intellectual and physical disability … thinking and dreaming and communicating in languages we do not understand … already expert in negotiating between two cultures … being nurtured in ways that challenge middle-class North American ideas about family. Educational research reminds us of the difficulties schools have encountered in providing for children of various skills, abilities and familial and socioeconomic backgrounds; other research stresses the link between the micro worlds of classrooms and the macro worlds of globalizing economies, in which historical inequities are reinforced and reproduced. Feminist work illustrates the inequities schooling contributes to in positioning girls differently from boys. In all, this research is not very encouraging as it continually points out that social inequities persist in all kinds of institutions, including schools.

As American teacher-educator Gloria Ladson-Billings put it:

Today teachers walk into urban classrooms with children who represent an incredible range of diversity. Not only are there students of different races and ethnicities but there are students whose parents are incarcerated or drug-addicted, whose parents have never held a steady job, whose parents are themselves children (at least chronologically), and who are bounced from one foster home to the next. And there are children who have no homes or parents. (Ladson-Billings, 2001: 14)

Ladson-Billings described two different challenges for urban teachers here. She pointed out the cultural, racial and linguistic diversity of students, and much of her book addresses how this kind of diversity might be a resource in classrooms. Ladson-Billings also pointed to profound social problems in the communities from which many students come. For teachers to recognize, respect, and when possible, cooperate with parents and communities to maintain diversity in the cultural, linguistic, religious, family constellations and other backgrounds of North American students is one challenge. Another is to develop ways of teaching that contribute to the extraordinary social change required to address the problems she identifies, as well as other pressing environmental, political, economic and social problems. As teachers working with our students every day, we know that we have to rely on more than our own past experiences in supporting our students and their families, and to contribute to necessary social change. The world is much more complicated than that.

Those of us who have made a commitment to teaching in this new century are acquainted first-hand with the diversity of our world and work hard to make our classrooms places where all can grow and learn. We believe that students who feel good about themselves – who feel strong and capable and competent as individuals – do better in school and generally in life. We also believe that students who participate in classroom activities – who feel comfortable and confident and needed in their classroom communities – do better in school and generally in life. We have these beliefs because we live intimately with students, day after day and year after year, and because we know that we ourselves are more effective teachers when we feel strong, capable, competent and members of communities. We want to do everything possible to create inclusive classroom communities that promote strong identities. But as we move through the demanding complexities of our days, it is difficult to tell whether our sincere intentions to provide optimal conditions for the growth of each student are being met. We worry that we are not doing the job we want to do. Why, despite our very best efforts, do some students continue to regard themselves as 'inadequate'? What prevents our classrooms from being the warm, caring and educative places we would like them to be for everyone, all of the time? What more can we do to make classrooms better places for all of us? What, if anything, do school 'systems' contribute to our unease with the outcomes of schooling? What, if anything, might Faculties of Education or educational researchers do about any of this?

Sometimes the problems that lead us to such questions become large enough to come to the attention to the world outside the school. Everyone has some awareness of turmoil in schools, and there is no shortage of advice. However, many of us are suspicious of the 'quick fixes' offered by publishers and their publicists in the form of yet another program complete with a thick teacher's guide and piles of supporting materials. We reject out of hand those politicians and bureaucrats who seek to create success by making failure illegal. We roll our eyes at those who look backwards to a fantasy time when everyone was the same and the rules all worked. We try to resist school staffroom colleagues who cite the numbers of ESL, disabled, single parent, transient, low income students and then throw up their hands in helpless despair – 'Well what can we do? It's not our fault!' These many voices are persistent and omnipresent. We hear them on TV and the radio and read them in newspapers and journals. We encounter them at teaching conferences and professional development days. Even at dinner parties and our own children's soccer games, we are lectured by people with simple answers to unbelievably complex issues.

As teachers, post-secondary educators and citizens, we know the sad results of the marginalizing of large numbers of our population. We know that teachers and schools need to do things differently – we need to speak to the multiplicity of voices and to the ambiguities and complexities we encounter in our classrooms. We need to understand our students differently, to stop defining them in terms of what they do not have or do not do, and instead, to discover and build on their strengths. We need new ways to look more closely and listen more carefully – ways that will open up new possibilities for our students and for ourselves. Most important, we need to believe in the possibility that things can change and be better.

The Teacher Action Research Group

It was essentially that search for something different that united the members of the Teacher Action Research Group, or TARG as we have come to call it, whose work we describe here. About 10 in number, we are in some respects a diverse group – elementary classroom teachers, adult education teachers, ESL specialists, student teachers, an Aboriginal teacher, university teachers, graduate students and a video ethnographer. Among us, we speak Punjabi, Bulgarian, French, Japanese and English.

There are more than 30 years between the youngest and oldest members. TARG met at Simon Fraser University (SFU) in a small, blue room with a large oval table in the middle, starting in 1999. We came together on Wednesdays at 4:00 from all over the Lower Mainland area of British Columbia – Vancouver, Burnaby, the Sechelt Peninsula, the Fraser Valley and even Bellingham, Washington.

We first met in September, 1999, when Kelleen Toohey, Professor of Education at SFU, invited us to form a group that would be concerned with 'investigating what practices in classrooms might make a difference to the learning of minority language background children' (Toohey, 1999). Kelleen's then newly published book, *Learning English at School: Identity, Social Relations and Classroom Practice* (*LEaS*) (Toohey, 2000) provided the base for our explorations. *LEaS* is an ethnographic study of a group of children of minority language backgrounds attending a Canadian school, from the beginning of kindergarten to the end of Grade 2. Identity construction practices, resource distribution and discourse practices together are shown to affect the children's possibilities for learning English. The book was primarily descriptive and theoretical and aimed at an academic audience. When it was being published, reviewers asked for explicit suggestions for changing school practices and Kelleen thought that teachers, better than she, could design practices in line with what she had found in the *LEaS* research. So she invited five elementary school classroom teachers, three graduate students and two ESL specialist teachers to help her with this design.

When the group first began to meet, we read and discussed a chapter of *LEaS* each week, bringing additional data, experiences and stories from our own classrooms, personal and professional lives, and experiences as variously situated educators. As we followed their progress through kindergarten, Grade 1 and Grade 2, the six focal children from *LEaS* were joined by the students whose stories TARG participants told, and we began to know each other and each other's students. In addition, we read Vivian Paley's (1993) *You Can't Say You Can't Play*, and it was extremely important in our developing shared understandings and commitments. Paley's attempts to make a rule against exclusion, captured in the title, resonated soundly with us and provided a standard both for looking at our own classrooms and for our work as members of TARG.

While the research proposal that initiated TARG indicated that the group would design, execute and analyze classroom practices that enabled better access to English by English language learners, the TARG classroom teachers, especially those who were more experienced, indicated that they were not interested just in designing or trying out particular practices in their classrooms to see if they 'worked'. Years of attending professional development workshops had dulled their enthusiasm for workable techniques. Instead, they were interested in deeper, more fundamental questions of their own. With focus on their own classrooms, they asked questions like: Who 'belongs' in classrooms? Who has power in classrooms? Do we really want all learners to be 'powerful'? Whose expectations are we assessing against when we say a student is meeting or is not meeting expectations on report cards? These broader questions were collaboratively discussed, and over time participants chose to engage in a variety of kinds of investigation of their questions. Some did academic research, some engaged in classroom action research, and others did 'reflective' research. We describe how we came to understand varieties of research practices in Chapter 2 of this book, and we discuss means we used that resulted in the research reports/stories in the following chapters.

The chapters that follow bring together written and spoken stories, published articles, conversations and academic and professional presentations of the members of TARG. Readers will note that some of the boxed stories presented here are research reports, but others are simply stories. Many researchers have described how teachers' knowledge is often represented in narratives, and TARG was no exception (e.g. Clandinin & Connolly, 2000). We started with consideration of a research report (*LEaS*), we added our own stories, some of us conducted systematic action research projects or reflective research and others did academic research. The book therefore, weaves together stories, commentary, our research and theoretical discussions. We have made no attempt to 'homogenize' the voices of our disparate members, or their various ways of representing their activities. Talking and working together through our differences has been an important part of our work together. We have enjoyed hearing how each of us speaks to our primary discourse communities – whether academic or professional. Experiencing how our various expertises are of use to the group, with no one of us having responsibility for being always a knower or always a learner, has been one of our many pleasures. We think this experience itself has shown us adults what kinds of learning communities we would like to create for our students, and we invite readers to imagine the same as they read this record of our work.

During the years of our meetings, some of us were graduate students and our classroom projects were topics for term papers or presentations at conferences; some completed degrees (Kathy Neilson, Suzanne Rowbotham, Chris Stewart and Joanne Thompson completed MAs with TARG-supported projects, and Bonnie Waterstone completed her PhD dissertation based on an analysis of the first year of our meetings); others published papers in academic or practitioner journals based on TARG projects; some attended meetings and participated actively but did not 'write up' their projects; we all gave presentations at scholarly and/or professional conferences. We saw this diversity in means of participation as entirely appropriate, as we worked toward creating an adult community that permitted and celebrated each member's varied participation in TARG. This book is our attempt to share with readers some of what we have come to understand about teaching and research, as we tell particular stories of students and ourselves in schools.

When we have looked back over the years of meetings, we have noticed that several themes have come up over and over during our discussions. There has been nothing fixed or scheduled or assigned about these themes, but they seem to echo throughout much of our work. We chat along and chat along and suddenly someone says, 'Hey look! We've actually been talking about *identity* again!' And just as easily and undeliberately as the themes have kept reappearing in our conversations, our understandings of them have changed and developed over time. The four themes (*identity, community and community practices, helping, possibilities*) are anything but distinct. They overlap and coexist and tangle. But they are important both as they relate to the work we do and as they relate to our group itself. They are areas in which the theoretical and practical, the university and public school worlds have come together to create both richer understandings of what is going on in education and possible directions for the future.

After examining in Chapter 2 what kinds of research TARG members engaged in (with special attention to teacher action research), we present aspects of our work together that illustrate how we came to understand the themes in Chapters 3, 4, 5 and 6. In Chapter 7, we discuss an issue that we think permeated TARG and many teacher and educational researcher lives, 'living in-between'. We conclude the book in Chapter 8.

The Themes

Identity

Identity was one of the themes that surfaced early in our discussions, as it was explicitly discussed in *LEaS*, and it provided a way for participants to talk about the varied social identities they, as well as their students, occupied. The concept of identity has been of great interest in contemporary scholarship in many fields, and the Canadian philosopher, Charles Taylor (1989), wrote a history of Western Europe's conceptions of identity, showing that the modern notion of each person having an enduring interior individual 'self', has not always characterized human beings' understandings of themselves, and does not universally represent how some cultures today understand themselves. The modernist view of human agents having individual characteristics that endure over time and stay the same in a variety of social milieu, has been critiqued by recent postmodern theorists (see Holland *et al.*, 1998; Norton, 2000; Weedon, 1987 for good descriptions of postmodern theories of identity). As Holland *et al.* (1998: vi) put it: 'Identities – if they are alive, if they are being lived – are unfinished and in process.' This postmodern conception of identity presents a complex picture of many 'selves' that vary depending on what context in which a person is located. Each context provides opportunities to act in particular ways and be a particular kind of person, and also has constraints so that one *cannot* act in certain ways nor be a certain kind of person there. Another aspect of contemporary understandings of identity is that persons actively struggle for agency – for ways to self-direct and make decisions that affect them – in situations that enable and constrain them in various ways. Holland *et al.* (1998: 5) remarked, 'Human agency may be frail, especially among those with little power, but it happens daily and mundanely, and it deserves our attention.' So, this contemporary view encourages us to pay attention to the situations in which persons take up identities, as well as the action persons take to assert agency in those situations. Such a view allows us to see students, for example, in complex ways, as we examine situations in which their agency is constrained or enabled, and the actions they take to assert that agency.

TARG members found vivid examples of this notion of complex identities as they contemplated the various selves they themselves occupied. They were teachers and university instructors, and had identities in their professional communities as such, but they were also mothers,[1] in life partnerships or not, daughters, sisters, friends and many other descriptors. Sometimes they noted how mixing up their various identities was confusing (e.g. one member talked about how odd it was to have her parents in the audience when she gave a scholarly talk – hard to be a daughter when being an academic). As TARG members contemplated their various roles or identities, they became aware of the different ways they were positioned in the communities that these identities, in a sense, reported to. The notion of *situated identities* (being a certain kind of person in specific situations) became clear to all, and TARG members also talked about how various activities or practices in their classrooms *positioned* both them and their students in particular ways. Many of the teacher participants, for example, critiqued the ways in which writing report cards positioned them as teacher-judgers and positioned their students as 'meeting or not meeting expectations'. They felt that report cards sabotaged their efforts to create democratic and healthy communities of learners in their classrooms. They felt they and their students could be different people when they were acting in community-of-learners ways, different from the ways they were positioned when doing report cards. They also talked about their struggles to make evaluations that positioned them and their students differently: as fellow travelers seeking ways to live and learn humanely.

So the notion of people having multiple identities and multiple possibilities became touchstones for TARG discussions about how teaching might contribute to other, more powerful identities for students (and teachers) who might not have such identities in school-as-usual. In Chapter 3, we explicitly tell 'identity stories', but it will be clear to readers, we think, that this theme runs throughout the book. We noted that identities were sometimes struggled for, and sometimes assigned, but that communities and their practices were important in what identities were available to people. Community and community practices thus became another important theme in our discussions.

Community and community practices

Like identity, community was a theme that emerged early in TARG discussions. In *LEaS*, the notion of 'communities of practice' (Lave & Wenger, 1991) was one of the structuring features of the research. Lave and Wenger drew attention with this phrase to the ways in which much human activity (including learning) occurs in relations among persons using particular tools, among particular communities. Unlike some, Lave and Wenger do not talk about the communities they were describing as unfailingly happy or democratic. Rather, they saw varieties of communities of practice, and looked at various apprenticeships as learning in communities of practice. Some of these apprenticeships (or communities) enabled newcomers to them to learn easily the practices of the community and to assume identities as experts, and others made it difficult to learn community practices and to attain identities of expertise. This social sense of learning has roots in the early 20th-century ideas of the Russian psychologist Lev S. Vygotsky (1978) and his colleagues. Vygotsky and other sociocultural theorists stressed that social relations and the tools people use are constructions of particular human communities and as such, they are specific and particular (and could always be other than what they are). As anthropologists, Lave and Wenger were aware that diverse human communities organized their social relations and tools in diverse ways and that attention to the specific ways of particular groups would help us see that there were no necessary or 'normal' or 'natural' ways of organizing social life. They also recognized that postmodern persons belong to many different and sometimes overlapping communities, and by participating in such communities, they learn diverse ranges of community practices. Attention to particular communities showed that participation in these practices was linked to the particular positions (or identities) of participants. A helpful article members of TARG read in this regard was Ray McDermott's (1993) cleverly titled paper, 'The acquisition of a child by a learning disability', in which he showed how some practices of schooling led to the inevitable result of labeling some children as more, and some as less, able. What was hopeful about this description, however, was that it need not necessarily be so, that with different practices, children did not have to be shown up as more and less able and that if we did not make (as he put it) such a *fuss* about the rate at which children learn, we might provide better environments for learners to participate and in so doing, get enough practice to become good at what they do.

In *LEaS*, the activities of six children who were learners of English as a second language over three years were described. Taking each classroom as a separate community, particular practices helped to construct various identities for each child. So, a child might have an identity in Grade 1 as a highly competent student, but in Grade 2 in a classroom with different practices, a child was constructed as an at-risk student. Similarly with regard to activities within the *same* classroom, a child might be seen as powerful builder of Lego structures, but be assigned (and perhaps claim) a completely different identity while being asked by the teacher to name letter sounds. This notion of communities and practices shaping who learners could be and what they could access as a result of who they were, became important as TARG members considered how teachers might effect change in classrooms.

Helping

Another important TARG theme emerged in our second year of meeting and that was the theme of help. As is discussed in Chapter 5 in more detail, we started to think about the ambiguities of helping as we discussed the buddy programs, peer tutoring, cooperative learning groups that others and we routinely set up in today's schools. We also considered how teaching was a form of helping students to be different from what they were before they came to us. Realizing the power teachers have in relationships with their students, we saw that 'helping', like most human interactions, always seems to entail power. Rogoff (2003) drew attention to the ways in which small local practices (like activities that happen in classrooms) often mirror far larger practices in society as a whole. We discussed often our perception that 'not needing help' (being powerful) seemed to be a valued position in societies as well as in classrooms, and how this value might be detrimental to the development of interdependent, thriving communities. Analyzing the power relations in help was the focus of one of our members Master's thesis (Thompson, 2002), and we examined data collected by Kelleen in one classroom in which children helping children was a valued practice, and in another in which children helping other children was a prohibited practice. As with respect to identity and community, we reached no firm conclusions about help, but came to see that our recognition of the com-plexities of help *helped us* to have rich conversations with one another about how classrooms and societies are organized. Far from being prescriptive about other people's practice, we came to see the importance of talking about these matters with colleagues.

Possibilities

Teachers … are positioned at a point of tension between seeing the necessity of things as they are and the persistent imagining of them turning out otherwise … of seeing at the same time the possibilities and the limits, the gains and the costs, the hopes, the disappointments, of any human endeavor. (Barbules, 1997: 66)

TARG members certainly wished to be persistent imaginers of how they might contribute to make things better for their students, their families and themselves. Like other teacher–researcher groups (examples include: Fishman & McCarthy, 2000; Jervis et al., 1996; Nunan, 1992; Zeichner & Noffke, 2001), members of TARG collaborated in attempting to make sense of things as they were in classrooms. Their conversations took a critical and political view of education, however, and were aimed not only at description and explanation but also change. We had the aim of moving both educational research and schooling practices toward more democratic and socially just goals (Cochran-Smith & Lytle, 1999).

Including the observations and insights of differently-situated educators in educational research has been seen by many as a way to produce more complete and nuanced descriptions of educational environments, and as a way to move teachers from being mere consumers of research to become participants in knowledge-making about their workplaces (Pappas, 1997). TARG was set up with such goals in mind, and the experience of working in such a research community has had impact on all participants in a variety of ways. Chapter 6 examines some of the possibilities teachers imagined for particular students and tells stories of hope for change in other similar communities. Reflecting on our own experiences within the TARG learning community strengthened our commitment to find better ways for children to learn and teachers to work in schools.

Living In-Between

Teachers recognized their classrooms as communities, but increasingly they began to understand the importance of seeing their classrooms as embedded in larger communities. One such community relevant to all was that of *school-as-system*, and teachers often said that they felt situated between children and the system. Teachers were critical of many of the system practices of school (and what school required of them as employees of bureaucracies). They thought these system practices often conflicted with their convictions that sometimes 'the rules' just did not work in their classrooms, or were detrimental to the education of the particular children with whom they worked. Novice and experienced teachers alike discovered that their discomfort and sometimes anger with some system practices were shared, and that many of these issues had been discussed in academic literature. With respect to research, teachers and the university-based participants sometimes found the same dilemma in their positioning in research sites between real people with real problems and the demands of scientific 'rigor'. Finding the vocabulary and allies to critique these practices was an unexpected boon of our work together. Chapter 7 discusses these issues.

Conclusion

Participatory action research groups come into existence around themes or topics that participants want to investigate, and they make a shared commitment to collaborating in action and research in the interests of transformation. They constitute themselves as a group or project for the purpose of mutual critical inquiry aimed at practical transformation of existing ways of doing things (practices/work), existing understandings (which guide them as practitioners/workers), and existing situations (practice settings/workplaces). (Kemmis & McTaggart, 2005: 585)

This book reports on our efforts to transform our practices, understandings and workplaces. We describe work that we have been engaged in as teachers and academics over the past few years in trying to understand how classrooms might be better for students of diverse linguistic and cultural backgrounds, abilities and socioeconomic circumstances, and better for teachers as well. We believe our work will be of interest to student teachers as they begin to consider the professional journeys they are embarking upon as they become newcomers to school and teacher communities. We also think it will be of interest to teachers and researchers who are interested in critically examining school practices, and in establishing communities of differently situated educators to discuss common problems and strategies. Allan Luke (2004: 1439) suggests we need 'a new community of teachers that could and would work, communicate and exchange – physically and virtually – across national and regional boundaries with each other, with educational researchers, teacher educators, curriculum developers, and indeed, senior educational bureaucrats'. Our experience with dialogue across occupational and other boundaries suggests that 'cosmopolitan dialogue' such as Luke described could be a fruitful way for teachers to rebuild teaching.

It is important to state that we do not here present a textbook, full of consistent advice or directions about what teachers or researchers must or must not do. Rather, we present our experiences, our research and our musings on those stories and research. We are convinced by what children's novelist Philip Pullman wrote: '"Thou shalt not" might reach the head, but it takes "Once upon a time" to reach the heart' (quoted in Miller, 2005: 1). We invite readers to consider our stories as they add their own stories of the classroom and students and trying to make things better.

Chapter 2
TARG Research Activities

These people might not have changed the world, but they have changed their worlds. Is that not the same thing?
Kemmis and McTaggart, 2005: 600

Introduction

In this chapter, we focus especially on teacher action research, variously named, and review literature that advocates, as well as criticizes, this approach. As will become clear, not all TARG research was action research, but a great deal of it was, and we discuss it most fully here.

Action research, usually taken to refer to research directed toward improving particular situations ('interested' research), has a very large literature. Denzin (2000) noted that such research has an almost 50-year history, with institutions of various sorts (social work, education, prisons and others) recognizing the power of research that aims not only at describing situations, but also at changing them. Long-time action research advocates Kemmis and McTaggart (2005) suggested that such research might have begun even earlier, with community development research in the United States in the 1930s. They and others have distinguished between action research, participatory research, critical action research, classroom action research and critical emancipatory participatory action research. In this chapter, we review some of the important descriptions of action research and situate TARG research activities within this wide array of activities.

Action Research in General

Nolen and Vander Putten (2007) recently argued that action research was a reaction to the need for relevant and practical knowledge in the social sciences; aimed at improving practice, action research involves researchers (who may or may not be insiders to the community whose practices are at issue) who systematically inquire into specified problems in specific situations, and search for changes to solve these problems. For many action researchers, this research was (and is) often collaborative and often has a critical, political and/or emancipatory commitment

(Fals Borda & Rahman, 1991; Freire, 1998). Unlike 'disinterested' researchers (if such a stance is even possible), action researchers do not claim objectivity, distance or lack of bias; instead, they go into their research fully conscious that their own perspectives and positions will have effects on their work. Action researchers want to make things better in a particular setting, and they attempt to make explicit their biases about what they think 'something better' is.

The objective of action research is change, and for many observers, an essential element of that process is dialog. Kemmis and McTaggart (2005: 578) described the critical, political, collaborative and active nature of action research groups as '*open[ing] communicative space* between participants', [a process which then creates] 'circumstances in which *collaborative social action* in history is ... justified by the force of better argument'. They relate action research projects to the communicative action intentions described by philosopher Jürgen Habermas (1996) in *Between Facts and Norms*: for Habermas, communicative action exists when a group questions the accuracy, sincerity, comprehension and/or moral appropriateness of a situation which they share. Habermas noted that raising such questions collaboratively builds solidarity in groups and strengthens the legitimacy of shared understandings, providing a platform for action planning.

Indeed, Habermas' (1989) discussion of 'public spheres' is a particularly apt way to examine the constitution of groups like TARG. For Habermas, a public sphere is 'made up of private people gathered together as a public and articulating the needs of society with the state' (Habermas, 1989: 176). Rutherford summarized Habermas' thought on the success of public spheres as depending on:

- the extent of access (as close to universal as possible);
- the degree of autonomy (the citizens must be free of coercion);
- the rejection of hierarchy (so that each might participate on an equal footing);
- the rule of law (particularly with respect to the subordination of the state);
- the quality of participation (the common commitment to the ways of logic). (Rutherford, 2000: 18)

In addition, Kemmis and McTaggart (2005: 584–591, passim, italics in original) note that 'As part of their inclusive character, public spheres tend to involve communication in *ordinary language*' and 'Public spheres frequently arise in practice [...] where voluntary groupings of participants arise in response to a legitimation deficit or a shared sense that a social problem has arisen and needs to be addressed'. We discuss how the concept of public sphere has relevance with respect to TARG activities below.

In the public sphere, as in action research groups, change is sought through persuasive argument. Such collectives are not in an 'us–them' relationship with authorities – the relationship is more complex and shifting. Neither public spheres or action research groups nor the bodies they oppose are unconflicted, unitary and autonomous; rather they are linked together in a social context that often includes shared goals and overlapping concerns. The systems that action research groups seek to change are often constraining but they may also be enabling. The aim of the transformative project is not to destroy institutions or systems but to oppose particular *practices* and to give compelling reasons for systems to change themselves.

We have found it helpful to examine TARG's activities through the lens of Habermas' concept of public sphere. We think TARG could be seen as a public sphere in its inclusivity, its commitment to honouring the diverse contributions of its differently situated participants, its attention to the practices of schooling and the necessity for them to change so as to provide adequate services to students who might differ from the mainstream in terms of language, cultural or ethnic background, abilities and so on. We describe TARG's activities in more detail later in this chapter.

Methods in Action Research

Kemmis and McTaggart's (2005) description of 'participatory action research' provided a relatively general description of action research methodology, and TARG research shares some of its characteristics. Noting the beginnings of such research as associated with social transformation movements in the Third World, Kemmis and McTaggart observed that typically, these action researchers were allied with particular ideologies in defining needed changes (Escobar, 1992; Fals Borda & Rahman, 1991; Freire, 1998). In terms of methodology, such research is nonlinear or 'spiral':

- Planning a change
- Acting and observing the process and consequences of the change
- Reflecting on these processes and consequences
- Replanning
- Acting and observing again
- Reflecting again, and so on ... (Kemmis & McTaggart, 2005: 563)

Important in participatory action research for them is the characteristic of 'shared ownership of research projects [involving] community-based analysis of social problems [with] an orientation toward community action' (Kemmis & McTaggart, 2005: 560). For them, action research is aimed at people searching together for 'more comprehensible, true, authentic, and morally right and appropriate ways of understanding and acting in the world. ... It is *a practice directed deliberately toward discovering, investigating, and attaining intersubjective agreement, mutual understanding, and unforced consensus about what to do* (Kemmis & McTaggart, 2005: 578, italics in original). Similarly, Wadsworth emphasized the collaborative nature of participatory action research:

> Essentially, Participatory Action Research (PAR) is research which involves all relevant parties in actively examining together current action (which they experience as problematic) in order to change and improve it ... [I]t tries to be a genuinely democratic or non-coercive process whereby those to be helped, determine the purposes and outcomes of their own inquiry. (Wadsworth, 1998: n.p.)

Some of the characteristics of participatory action research are true of teacher action research, while others (especially the notion of collective action in any particular site) are not so commonly found in educational settings. A teacher's daily isolation in her own classroom means that teacher research often has a somewhat less consensual and mutual focus than the activist workplace-, community-based projects other writers describe. We return to this issue of collective action with respect to TARG later in this chapter.

Teacher Action Research, Classroom Research, Teacher Inquiry, Teacher Self-Study: It is Still Rock 'n' Roll to Me

The methodology of action research has become common in educational research over about the last 20 years. Nolen and Vander Putten noted that 'Educators see it as a practical yet systematic research method to investigate their own teaching and their students' learning in and outside the classroom' (Nolen & Vander Putten, 2007: 401). Employing the same cycles of observation, reflection, intervention, data gathering and reflection as described for participatory action research, this educational inquiry involves teachers in considering how classroom conditions might be improved. Denzin observed that classroom action research is usually characterized by 'qualitative, interpretive modes of inquiry and data collection by teachers (often with help from academics) with a view toward teachers making judgments about how to improve their own practices' (Denzin, 2000: 569). Denzin further observed that such work is 'practical in Aristotle's sense of practical reasoning about how to act rightly and properly in a situation with which one is confronted' (Denzin, 2000: 569).

Cochran-Smith and Lytle characterized teacher-directed investigation of practice as 'taking an inquiry stance' toward practice:

> Teachers and student teachers who take an inquiry stance work within inquiry communities to generate local knowledge, envision and theorize their practice, and interpret and interrogate the theory and research of others. Fundamental to this notion is the idea that the work of inquiry communities is both social and political; that it involves making problematic the current arrangements of schooling; the ways knowledge is constructed, evaluated and used; and teachers' individual and collective roles in bringing about change. (Cochran-Smith & Lytle, 1999: 289)

El-Haj (2003) described the powerful impact of an informal urban teacher network, the Teachers' Learning Cooperative (TLC), for example, that engaged teachers in weekly meetings to participate together in social and political inquiry into the current arrangements of schooling. El-Haj reported that TLC developed 'a set of oral inquiry processes that use observation and description of the particular as the foundation from which to create rich, innovative curriculum and pedagogy' (El-Haj, 2003: 818). She further argued for the validity of collaboratively constructed teacher knowledge and its power to transform not only the situations of students and teachers in individual classrooms but also the formulation and application of educational policies on a broader basis. She argued that the deeply reflective and collaborative inquiry into 'the particular' that TLC members engaged in attended effectively to 'the multiplicity, complexity, and uncertainty that characterize human learning' (El-Haj, 2003: 819.) She also noted: 'It is through an analysis of the particular that the conditions that produce inequality are revealed and that practices aimed at social change are developed' (El-Haj, 2003: 819). Members of this group did not formally engage in the recognized/traditional/academic qualitative research process, but through oral sharing of detailed data collection focused on single children and through structured conversational strategies, these teachers examined, questioned, reframed and transformed their teaching practice.

The term 'self-study' has also been used to describe teacher action research – with focus on the particular individual setting of a single classroom and a teacher's individual pedagogy. Taking action is still an important component of this research, but deeply personal reflective questions lie at the heart of it. As Samaras and Freese put it:

> Self-study respects the notion that we teach who we are and who we are becoming as professionals. Teachers ask themselves questions such as, 'How did I arrive at the assumptions, dispositions and attitudes I have about teaching and learning' ... The process of self-study is a practice of self-directed professional development and it has a self-monitoring nature. Critical friends, with alternative views, improve the process (Bass *et al.*, 2002; Wilcox *et al.*, 2004). As self-study teachers make their research known to others, they share a commitment to better understanding their practice. (Samaras & Freese, 2006: 48)

Samaras and Freese pointed out two aspects of this teacher research we have not yet discussed: the presence of 'critical friends' and the presentation of teacher research to others. We in TARG certainly benefited from the dialog with 'critical friends' (one another) to help us design, frame and improve our teaching and research practices. We also found presentations of various sorts helped focus our efforts.

How did TARG Proceed?

In Chapter 1, we described a little of how TARG began its work. Our initial activity was reading several texts and articles, and discussing them, to forge ourselves as a community with some shared experience and knowledge. The teachers in the group responded to the readings with stories of their own – about students in their present and past classes, about their own children and about themselves as children and as teachers.

In most descriptions of teacher inquiry groups, observers recount how teachers tell stories about children and classrooms. The sharing of stories is the currency of such groups' discourse, although these particularities are often understood to be representative of larger issues of systemic policy, philosophy and design. TARG teacher members told stories of what they perceived as beneficial, harmful or even just silly school practices. They told stories about particular students, about their own children, and about themselves. Often, the point of bringing in a story was to have the group's help in understanding a particular situation or student more fully and in considering ways that practices might change in order to support the student's success. Sometimes the stories led directly toward questions that underlay teachers' individual research projects. These stories were expressed, of course, in ordinary language and readers will find transcripts of those stories throughout this book.

The phrase 'You can't say you can't play' from Paley's (1993) book became an important norm for TARG. Membership was not limited, and after the initial invitation, more people were invited to join and did over the years. Membership fluctuated somewhat, with some leaving the group and more joining. As in Habermas' imagined public sphere, our intent was to be as inclusive as possible of varying viewpoints.

The aims and processes of TARG, The Learning Community (TLC) and other 'inquiry communities' share many parallels. First, for many groups, including TARG, the ultimate goal is the inclusion of all students, to find ways to respect the individual strengths and values of each student within a system that is designed to promote the success of certain students and ensure the failure of others. In TARG, the quest for equity for English language learners, students with special needs, and others, drove weekly conversations and participants' individual projects. The focus was on changing practice (or schools) rather than on how students or students' families must change. As Paley put it:

> The [traditional] approach has been to help the outsiders develop the characteristics which will make them more acceptable to the insiders. I am suggesting something different: The group must change its attitudes and expectations toward those who, for whatever reasons, are not yet part of the system. (Paley, 1993: 33)

Reading Paley, some TARG members expressed their appreciation for her clear articulation of a notion they had intuited, but had been unable to formulate previously.

In about the middle of our first year, the teachers in the group were encouraged to articulate questions of interest to them in classrooms, and then the whole group would try to aid each teacher in articulating her questions, designing ways to investigate these questions and collaborating both in analyzing collected data and in 'writing-up' results of the research. Each project was directed by the teacher who initiated it, while the university researchers (the graduate students, the video ethnographer and Kelleen) suggested theoretical and/or empirical work as well as logistical issues to the teachers to consider when forming their questions, gathering and analyzing data. Sometimes the graduate students consulted with the teachers about their writing, but mostly the group as a whole responded to the ongoing reports of the projects. Over the course of the years, some TARG members completed several projects, while others chose to delve ever more deeply into the same questions that had motivated them at the start. The graduate students and Kelleen also shared their own research and writing with the group, which was not 'action research', but more traditional qualitative research with systematic data collection and analysis.

University researcher–teacher collaboration in educational research has sometimes been argued as potentially more powerful than 'disinterested' research in that more data is available when teachers' insights are included, and in that data analysis can be more multifaceted with teacher participants. The proportion of teacher involvement in 'collaborative' research has varied – some projects fully involve teachers in research design, data collection, analysis and presentation, and other projects involve teachers more or less fully in some but not all, stages of the research. However, the responsibility for the research is often not the teacher's, and they typically become somewhat like informants or research assistants. TARG was a bit different: teachers were in charge of their own projects and they got assistance from the university-based members who suggested other work they might consult. Reciprocally, the teachers in the group would aid the university researchers providing their knowledge from closer experience in schools to aid in design of important questions, feasible data collection procedures and insights for data analysis. And, as we have already mentioned, the final presentation of the teachers' research (its 'writing-up') differed from member to member; although we all gave presentations at professional and academic conferences, some were content to present their research on particular topics just to the group; others chose to publish their work in practitioner and academic journals, and some of us completed papers for courses and theses. As in the classrooms for children we imagined, members could participate in this small adult community in whatever ways were comfortable for them.

One TARG activity that we did all participate in that was decidedly not comfortable for some members was the oral presentations we gave. Some of the teachers, in particular, who had little experience speaking before large groups of adults, expressed anxiety about this, especially in our first presentations. However, with group support and practice, even these members became somewhat more comfortable with the activity and described their participation as difficult, but 'good for them'.

Was the Teacher Research, Research?

For TARG members the weekly conversations served multiple purposes – questions and doubts about the research process itself were articulated and sometimes resolved; thinking was clarified; resources were shared; new ideas, new perspectives, and new directions were encountered, considered and established. Groups like TARG and TLC are of great benefit to teachers and to some children, but can these conversational meetings, and informally represented projects, really be considered research? In our view, such conversations are powerful examples of the collaborative processes of action research. Underlying the informal register of the dialogue is a process that mirrors that of traditional/academic research: the participants begin with a question; data is collected and shared; the data is collaboratively analyzed and interpreted; conclusions are drawn or new learning is articulated. Although it is conducted on a small scale and its representation often takes place in intimate settings – and usually leads to action rather than to presentation or publication – we think that the collaborative process in which we engaged was a genre of educational research that is important, valid and innovative.

Whether we label it teacher inquiry, classroom-based inquiry, action research or self-study, the process of investigation undertaken by TARG, TLC and millions of other teachers in professional learning communities fulfils the definition of action research proposed by Kemmis and McTaggart: disciplined study that is collaborative, local, problem- or practice-based, politically informed and transformational. El-Haj (2003: 827) located the work that TLC members did as 'within a broader philosophical tradition that envisions education as a site for liberatory practices aimed at the development of democratic culture in which each person is recognized and valued (Carini, 2001; Dewey, 1916; Freire, 1998; Greene, 1988)'. From this perspective, the work of teacher TARG members was research.

Other theorists see it differently. Freebody (2003) saw the particularity of action research as problematic. He critiqued much action research as 'analytically light' (Freebody, 2003: 88). He acknowledged the high degree of care taken in most action research *design* and in – especially – the conduct of the researcher in relation to the researched. However, he claimed that thorough data analysis is often lacking, that there is little application of known, established and appropriate data analysis methods. This limits the resulting knowledge to remain applicable only within its own context.

Bodone (2005) echoed Freebody's claim that working teachers do not have enough time to do sufficiently thorough data analysis, and that their work is therefore limited to their local context. She claimed that basing research exclusively on teacher knowledge can create, 'a romantic view of experiential knowledge' (Bodone, 2005: 121). She argued for a new kind of dialog that fused insider and outsider knowledge, claiming that each perspective needs the other to see its own inadequacies.

We agree in part with these critiques, but we believe that the question of whether teachers do or do not do research is unnecessary. Teachers and academics engage in different practices in their workplaces, and writing extended prose is not one of teachers' customary school activities. The productions of the teacher members of TARG (with the exception of their theses) were not academic, but this is not to say they did not have what Lather (1991) calls 'catalytic validity' in changing these teachers' minds, or in contributing to educating others. The standards by which teacher action research is judged may have more to do with aesthetic and catalytic properties than scientific rigor. In the end, we decided that we were not so interested in defending teacher research as Research, as we were in investigating what might result from academics and teachers sharing their insights into schools. We accepted the notion that the world of academic research and the world of teaching each had benefits to offer the other, resulting in a university researcher–teacher relationship that was quite fluid. Acknowledging the variety of work practices of members, and recognizing that teachers and the university researchers spoke to different primary discourse communities, TARG members came to learn that while some projects in which we were involved were traditional academic research, other projects were best suited to discourse within practitioner communities. Readers will see the variety of types of products TARG developed throughout this book.

Conclusion

El-Haj (2003: 833) summarized some of the benefits of teacher research by observing that 'even though the Teacher Learning Collective's processes are often grounded in observations of particular children, the knowledge generated and accumulated over time holds broad implications for educational practice'. Educational action researchers examine their values, beliefs and practices through reflection, dialogue, and investigations into previous research, and then take action to transform practices from within, to seek to influence policy by persuasion, where possible. As already mentioned, TARG members did not only do teacher action research, but involved participants in considering academic research as well. We think that an important contribution of TARG is that we showed how teacher action researchers benefited from close work with academic researchers in seeing models of qualitative research, but also that the academic researchers benefited tremendously from participating peripherally in teacher action research, and seeing their attention to individuals and the particular. For both the action and academic researchers, we think the collaboration improved one another's work. As Radnor put it:

> Researching the interpretive way in educational settings ... engages us, in a deep sense, in articulating our reflections of practice. By understanding that reality is interpreted experience, and by confronting, through the research process, how we interpret our own lived experience and that of others, we empower ourselves to try to transform aspects of our lives. (Radnor, 2002: 119–120)

Chapter 3
Identity

Raminder's Story

Joanne Thompson

Last year I worked with a kindergarten student who taught me about patience and about what can happen when teachers set aside timelines and comfort zones and work together as questioning professionals. Raminder was 3'1" and weighed 28 pounds. Her birthday was in December, which meant that she started her kindergarten year when she was four years old. She was the youngest, shortest and most fragile-looking child in her class. Sometime during the spring before starting school, Raminder had been hit by a truck and spent four months in a hip to toe cast recovering from a fractured femur and a dislocated hip. Common classroom activities such as sitting upright with legs crossed fatigued her. Sometimes she looked as though she was engaged, and at other times she seemed to be staring into space. Most noticeably, however, Raminder was silent. Her silence appeared to be real – not contrived, not manipulative. While she occasionally subvocalized to a select few children, all of her classmates were quick to volunteer, 'Raminder doesn't talk. I can tell you what she wants.'

To complicate matters, English was Raminder's second language, her first being Punjabi. Her family had enrolled her in a full day kindergarten available for ESL students where she had two different teachers – one in the morning and a different one in the afternoon. The morning teacher thought that when Raminder became comfortable within the classroom setting, she would begin to speak. The afternoon teacher was distressed by her silence and 'lack of normal interaction' and, within the first month of school, had called a school-based team meeting to ask for Raminder's removal from school, saying,

Continued

'Perhaps she can return next year when she is socially, emotionally and linguistically ready.' As a member of the school-based team, I disagreed and was convinced that Raminder and her parents had a right to public education. After discussion, Raminder stayed in kindergarten.

Several months later, I was called to the administrator's office and told that both teachers were now concerned that Raminder was still not speaking voluntarily. They questioned whether or not Raminder should repeat Kindergarten the next year. I reminded the principal that Raminder's parents had consented to a complete medical check by her pediatrician and that the Public Health nurse had completed a developmental assessment with the assistance of a translator. Both the doctor and the health nurse had reported no abnormalities, no pathologies and no label other than 'normal'. I told him that I had arranged a home visit with Raminder and her parents. He asked me to report back regarding my opinion on Raminder repeating kindergarten.

So the morning kindergarten teacher, a translator and I went to visit our silent little Raminder. We watched while she skipped into the kitchen, poured herself a bowl of cereal and argued with her brother over who got the most marshmallow bits. While her father explained to the adults how much Raminder loved school – how she was learning to take risks like going down the big slide and how she wasn't able to stop smiling about her new experiences, Raminder picked up her brother's Grade 1 reading book and displayed all the skills in Marie Clay's reading readiness assessment. She opened the book, turned it right side up and turned pages from front to back looking at pictures, pretending to track the words from left to right with her finger, and whispering made-up words to the story. She was a relaxed little girl, albeit quiet, busying herself while adults talked. She looked at her teacher with huge brown eyes and smiled. They sat next to each other, sharing the book, and whispered and nodded and pointed.

The next morning I received this e-mail from the kindergarten teacher.

I'm sure her name means something like 'a treasured ruby' or some such poetic thing ... little Raminder was such a lady today! I sensed for the first time, a long-lashed, eye-contacting, soul-contacting little girl! If she was speaking today, it was DEFINITELY with those eyes: THIS is MY house ... you are sitting on MY couch ... this is MY best friend,

Continued

MY brother ... just about everybody who loves me in this world is in MY LIVING ROOM!

Joanne, when I drove away, there was Raminder still standing against the bottom half of her screen door, but she gave me the HUGEST smile as I turned the corner and waved! I couldn't help but wave ... it was like HELLO instead of Goodbye! What a wonderful child. What wonderful parents and grandparents ... am I ever glad we visited. I shall be doing home visits when the new school year starts, thanks to sitting alongside Raminder this afternoon. It will help me to walk again in interesting places. I watched her entire body today ... I listened and I watched. I had temporarily forgotten that phonemic awareness is only secondary to getting on the Big Slide at the Big School and making ourselves smile Big. I must go now and do some checklists on report cards ... 'is meeting', 'is not meeting', 'is exceeding' expectations ... where is the column that says just good old 'IS'?

TARG member Joanne Thompson is an experienced English as a Second Language specialist and Speech and Hearing Pathologist who works with individuals, small groups and teachers both in and out of the classroom. In her notes for a TARG presentation to student teachers, Joanne showed that moving to a 'different space' provided a dramatically different view of Raminder. TARG members were moved by Raminder's Story, and during the lengthy discussions that followed we found ourselves returning over and over to the importance of going into, what we came to call, 'different spaces'. As Joanne said during a discussion:

Raminder's Story is about the power of language and the impact of assigning identities. It is also about how comfortable we are in staying the same. Perhaps that is because we do not have time to do otherwise, but in order to know Raminder more fully, we had to step out of our four classroom walls and go into somebody else's environment – a place where we were somewhat uncomfortable and she was not.

Sharing time with children whose cultural backgrounds are different from our own, and who speak languages other than those we know, is, as we have already said, a privilege and a challenge for teachers. A privilege because in the intimacy of the classroom and the relationships it fosters, teachers and other students have the opportunity to understand in more than touristic ways, other ways of speaking, feeling and doing.

A challenge because learning is rarely comfortable, and discovering that one's beliefs are not universally held is, well, challenging. Yet we know that we have to get to know our students and their families and that the more we know about their strengths, interests, experiences and beliefs, the better we will be able to meet their educational needs and provide the environments in which they can learn.

The Little Girl, Raminder and other members of our shared classroom provoked far-ranging discussions during which we realized that many of the dilemmas we experience in our classrooms have something to do with the ways our students see themselves, the ways they are seen by others, and the effect of those views on classroom behavior and achievement. We kept rediscovering that 'learners' identities have definite and observable effects on what they can do in classrooms, what kinds of positions ... in classrooms they can occupy, and therefore, how much they can learn' (Toohey, 2000: 74). Identities are complex: on the one hand, they are how a person sees herself, but they are also how a person is positioned by others. Not only are identities then constructed from within and from without, they are multiple, because persons are engaged in a variety of different social environments, in which their identities might be variously constructed. The parts teachers and schools play in determining the identities students are assigned or take on, the ways in which identity negotiation functions in classrooms, and the effect of those identities on participation are all aspects of one of the recurring themes in our TARG discussions.

It is unfortunately the case that many children in today's classrooms quickly acquire identities that are seen as problematic. TARG members had no shortage of examples to discuss. The stories that follow illustrate some of the puzzles teachers confront daily in our classrooms. Kelleen Toohey's notes for an academic presentation follow the path taken by Surjeet, a girl who entered kindergarten as a seemingly competent English-speaking student and by Grade 3 had been designated ESL and a 'limited' learner. Surjeet was one of the six focal students in Kelleen's *LEaS*. As she followed Surjeet through her first three years in school, Kelleen watched her become less and less successful. Here, readers are given the opportunity to see some of the factors that contributed to the development of Surjeet's school identity. According to Kelleen, 'compulsory kindergarten attendance marks a substantial shift in how children's behavior, growth and development are assessed and compared with others. Although children come to kindergarten as kinds of children, very quickly they attain identities as kinds of students ...' (Toohey, 2000: 96)

Assigning Marginality: The Case of an ESL/LD Student

Kelleen Toohey

More than 20 years ago, educational anthropologist Margaret LeCompte observed that children entering kindergarten have to learn a 'bundle of tasks ... the attitudes and values which surround being a student'. She called instilling these tasks, attitudes and values, 'civilizing' children. She saw children becoming students as a benign and required transition in which they learn how to be managed by teachers and others. She writes:

> Part of learning the student role involves altering children's relationship with adults. No longer are adults primarily parents who provide nurture; rather, they include teachers and others who impose more uniform and objective standards for behavior. (LeCompte, 1980: 105)

I would like to examine how it is that we identify children through these 'uniform and objective' standards in schools. Benign 'uniform and objective standards of behavior' does not describe the school practices I observed in a study conducted in the late 1990s in a Canadian school. Rather, it seemed to me that those practices increasingly during the early years of school, worked to rank children on behaviors and tasks that were arbitrary, interested and far from uniform or objective. These practices created particular identities or ranks for children, identities that became seen as social facts.

Briefly, my ethnographic study followed two cohorts of English language learners from minority language backgrounds (ESL learners) attending a school in the Lower Mainland, from kindergarten entrance to the end of their Grade 2 year (Toohey, 2000). The school is in a suburban working-class neighborhood. About 50% of the children at the school have a home language other than English, representing a wide variety of languages. In particular, I focus on one child, whom I call Surjeet, the oldest child of an immigrant Punjabi Sikh family. She lives with her parents, a younger sibling, grandparents, an aunt and older cousins in a house not far from the school. The family uses both Punjabi and English at home, but on the advice of her grandfather (a retired school principal from India), Surjeet's parents, grandparents and aunt speak only English with the children. Surjeet's grandfather

Continued

planned to teach the children Punjabi and Punjabi literacy after they had learned to read in English. Thus, Surjeet entered kindergarten as an English-dominant child, knowing, in her mother's words, 'only a few words of Punjabi'. However, at an English interview with the kindergarten teacher before her entry to school, Surjeet was reticent and shy (not unlike many children). It may be because she was so quiet, her teacher designated her as 'ESL' and consequently, she was enrolled in a special afternoon 'Language Development' kindergarten program, in addition to the 'regular' morning program. Thus, Surjeet's first school identity position, ESL, did not accurately describe her use of English or Punjabi.

Initially, Surjeet had some difficulties, again, as do many children, with starting kindergarten. Every morning she cried when her mother left her at school. However, she quickly began to interact with the other children, and many of those interactions appeared pleasurable and playful. With Donna, another anglophone, Surjeet had many such conversations, and together, they played with other children who spoke English. When Surjeet was involved in disputes with other children (common in playgroups), her participation was lively and sometimes effective in that she gained access to disputed play materials or deflected potentially insulting comments. As well, she participated more and more actively and comfortably in choral activities: counting, chanting, singing and so on. Like many children, in choral activities, Surjeet was initially quite unsure and silently mouthed the alphabet or numbers or seasons and so on. With the daily repetition, however, she soon became very verbally active in classroom choral work. I regularly observed Surjeet's obvious skill with memory tasks and reading while she played with other children. She also read the signs and labels around the classroom to other children and to me, in a 'show-off' display of literacy in which many children engaged. My video data also show Surjeet assisting other children in reading. She showed sensitivity to other children, appearing uncommonly aware of her classmates, and participating competently in the classroom 'dance'. Unfortunately, her teacher rarely witnessed her competence. For whatever reasons, when her teacher was present, Surjeet typically was very quiet and inactive.

After the winter break, Surjeet's relatively easy access to many of the children in the room appeared to decline. Her close association with Donna ceased. Other children began usurping her place in the room,

Continued

dismissing her and excluding her from their play. As the school year wore on, fewer children were friendly with her. Surjeet became positioned in conversations as someone who was not believed and who was not allowed a conversational place. Children told her to get out of seats they wanted, and to surrender play materials; they ignored her and her attempts at counter-discourse were unsuccessful. Her teacher told me in April that Surjeet appeared to be having social difficulties, and she wondered what Surjeet might be doing to cause these.

Interestingly, Surjeet's social difficulties coincided with the beginning of a new instructional practice: an early literacy activity called 'reading the morning message'. In this circle activity, the teacher asked individual children to pick out letters or words in a short message written on the chalkboard. These were 'solo' performances, and competence as a solo performer seemed a way of gaining a 'smart child' identity. Surjeet almost never volunteered to be a participant in the practice, although she did participate in the choral reading of the message after the individual performances.

In play activities, choral speech and singing, children have the opportunity to use others' language and knowledge, as well as play materials as resources for their performances. In group interactions early in the school year, Surjeet appeared good enough linguistically and cognitively to participate actively. However, in solo activities when the teacher's and other children's resources were unavailable to her, Surjeet sometimes appeared cognitively disorganized and linguistically incoherent. She also displayed this kind of incoherence in conversations with unfriendly children.

Some of Surjeet's classmates who were also designated ESL, 'graduated' from ESL by the end of kindergarten, but Surjeet's identity as an ESL student was solidified by then. Her performance in May of kindergarten on a test with the school's ESL specialist teacher, whom Surjeet did not know, was minimal and somewhat incoherent. Consequently, the ESL teacher and her kindergarten teacher recommended that she should receive specialist pull-out ESL teacher support in Grade 1.

At the beginning of Grade 1, Surjeet was particularly interested in journal writing and she produced a great deal of the inexperienced emergent writing common at this age. Her delight with this new activity, writing her experiences down, was apparent to me, and I felt hopeful that her teacher would notice her enthusiasm and build upon it.

Continued

However, the class period for journaling soon became the period in which the school specialist ESL teacher pulled children from the classroom for oral ESL instruction. Surjeet therefore missed journal writing, and thereafter, her skills in writing in English developed slowly.

Over the course of Grade 1, both instructional practices and assessment practices increasingly required Surjeet to perform solo, and she appeared increasingly uncomfortable with such performances. At the end of Grade 1, her teacher felt Surjeet's language delays, caused by her 'ESLness', might be complicated with learning and cognitive delays. But she was promoted to Grade 2 nevertheless, with a note in her file that the Grade 2 teacher might want to watch for evidence of delay.

Surjeet's Grade 2 teacher used a common practice, the Initiation, Response, Evaluation sequence in which the teacher asks a question, picks children to answer and then evaluates their answers. This teacher often asked Surjeet to answer (although, or maybe because, Surjeet seldom volunteered). Frequently, she failed to supply the answers wanted by her teacher and remained silent. These humiliating episodes presented Surjeet as incompetent, not only to the teacher but also to other students.

Surjeet's Grade 2 teacher believed quite early in the school year that Surjeet was 'limited' or a slow learner in addition to her problems with English, and she felt these problems would 'dog Surjeet all her life'. Her estimate of Surjeet's abilities did not change during the year. Despite her average score on a standardized achievement test administered in May, the Grade 2 teacher recommended Surjeet for Learning Assistance toward the end of Grade 2. Surjeet was then tested, again by a specialist teacher she did not know, and this teacher concurred that she had learning problems. Therefore, in Grade 3, Surjeet was removed from her regular classroom, not only for ESL instruction, but also for Learning Assistance.

My data illustrate circumstances that positioned Surjeet in particular ways in her various classrooms and in various practices. Anthropologist Ray McDermott (1993: 293) has said that some classroom activities, 'organize a search for differential performance ... to organize the degradation of those found at the bottom of the pile'. Recognizing that children learn at different rates, McDermott argued that if 'less fuss' were made about this, children might not have to be concerned about degradation and that their learning might be enhanced accordingly.

Continued

Identifying ESL students upon entry to kindergarten was the first practice to assign 'differential performance' to children in Surjeet's cohort. Counting ESL students is a necessary (and contested) practice in schools in this province because increased funding accompanies the designation. Schools with high ESL populations thus have resources not available to other schools. However, creating a category of ESL as problematic, creates the trap into which Surjeet fell: her reticence, together with the prevailing instructional and evaluation practices of her classroom, caused teachers to consistently underrate her linguistic and cognitive achievements and potential.

What Surjeet learned at school was how to be more silent, to venture opinions less often, to agree with the more powerful and to limit her attempts to appropriate her community's linguistic and other resources. Her defensive speaking strategies were evaluated as incoherence. Surjeet's language problems, far from resulting from internalized learning 'traits' or disabilities, were produced, in a sense, by the organization of classroom events.

I have not discussed at all in this counter-account of Surjeet anything to do with her cultural background or the resources of her community, whose knowledge, stories, practices and values did not, and perhaps could not, accompany her to school. What is considered knowledge in schools is socially and culturally specific. Indeed, some children will be advantaged and others disadvantaged by this. But practices in classrooms that place children in positions in which they must protect their identities, or get under the radar, that place them alone for all to judge, jeopardize many children's educational journeys, not only children whose family practices differ from those of the school.

As we have seen here, assigning children identities as inadequate performers makes their access to the activities that might make them improve their performances increasingly remote. Problematically, the current enthusiasm for accountability – increased attention to practices for differentiation of individuals in school, not only does nothing to erase those differences, but actively contributes to the construction, maintenance, growth and hegemony of such differences. Measuring children's differences assuming that they indicate 'problems', and totting up how many children have such problems is accounting, not accountability. Accountability consists of understanding what is really happening with children and making sure that classroom practices afford them suitable learning environments.

The practices that contributed to the identification of Surjeet as a problem student, are considered up-to-date, standard practices. Most teachers would agree that one of the first and most important tasks of the school year is to assess their students. In fact, observing children was probably one of our first assignments as student teachers. Using anecdotal notes, checklists, tests, grids, formal standards, lists of expectations, specialists, codes and more to help, we look for strengths, weaknesses and individual differences. We have learned that we must figure out what 'kinds of students' we have this year – which kids are younger and which are older, which are 'talkers' and which are quiet, those who have spoken only English and those who are learning English as an additional language, which have had pre-school or day care experience and which are leaving their families for the first time, which can hold a pencil and use scissors properly and which know the alphabet. We know that every class will have a wide range of abilities and skill levels, and we want to know where each child falls within that range – those who are relatively independent and those who will need extra support. We trust that if we can determine the unique features of each child – the learning style, the personality type, the social position, the 'intelligence', we can be more effective in reaching every child. We have been taught that if we can determine early which children will have difficulty succeeding in school, we will have a better chance of fixing whatever problems exist. As in health care, we believe 'early detection' provides the best chances for cures. Our purpose is to assess the needs both of the class and of individuals. Once that is done, we can begin working to meet those needs. But, as the Surjeet story illustrates, our diagnoses have ambiguous results.

Holland *et al.* (1998) point out that the decisions teachers make about who students are have major effects on who students can be, and what they can learn in classrooms:

> Even in situations where all students are admitted to an arena of learning, learning is likely to become unevenly distributed in its specifics. Teachers will take some students' groping claims to knowledge seriously on the basis of certain signs of identity. These students they will encourage and give informative feedback. Others, whom they regard as unlikely or even improper students of a particular subject ... are less likely to receive their serious response. (Holland *et al.*, 1998: 27)

The authors here point out that inclusion is more than a desk in a classroom – that students' identities are profoundly important in their access to knowledge in classrooms. Valerie Walkerdine (1998) conducted research in Australia that suggested that even when girls achieved similar results on mathematics examinations as boys, their achievements were minimized and dismissed as 'only following rules', not engaging in the creative activities of mathematical thinking (which boys, as 'rule-breakers' did engage in). Presumably, the girls' 'groping claims to knowledge' were not taken as seriously as the boys'.

Identity assignment is a central practice of schools. Reporting to students, parents, administrators and ultimately, the state, about the learning achievements of students is part of a teacher's job. We do these assessments for practical and caring reasons. We are aware of the diversity within our classrooms and want the children in our care to be successful. We have been given huge responsibilities and we take them very seriously. But at the same time, we need to be aware that we are also participating in a very pervasive and powerful process that ranks and positions our students – and that this process itself can produce significant, long-lasting damage. Surjeet is but one example. ESL, slow, bright, artistic, behavior problem, ADHD, good, difficult, Learning Disabled, young, advanced, challenged … are only some of the labels (or identities) informally and formally applied to children in our classes as we sift and sort and try to figure out how to proceed. But identities, once assumed or assigned, are difficult to change. Once a child has been ranked and assigned an identity, teacher attitudes towards the child and their assigned identity become factors in the access the child has to his community and the resources within it.

It is unsettling to think that the identities children are assigned or 'get' in schools may be damaging to them. We wonder not only what factors contribute to the acquisition of such identities but, more importantly, what we can do to change them. When TARG members were choosing topics for their first research projects, primary grade teacher Corey Denos (2003) said that she wanted to take the opportunity to look at something in her classroom that had frustrated and irritated her for years – specifically the bullying behavior of some girls towards other girls. In the following condensation of a paper published in the professional magazine *Language Arts* (July 2003), Corey describes changes that took place in her awareness, understanding and attitude as she focused her attention on one child with a problematic identity.

Jennifer: Negotiating Powerful Positions in a Primary Classroom[2]

Corey Denos

> *This morning the children trooped cheerily into the classroom, stomping snow off their boots, unbuttoning, zipping, tying, buckling jackets and snow*

Continued

pants, and chattering about snowmen and slipping on the ice and what was on TV last night. Within a few minutes most of them had found books and friends and were sprawled on the carpet or hunched on the teaching bench or sitting around tables.

But what's this? Teresa is crying. Her eyes are downcast and so sad. Her fingers are in her mouth. Tears spill silently down her face. As usual she says nothing, but an interested bystander states that Teresa has no friends. That no one is going to play with her.

Says who?

All eyes shift to Jennifer and Selina who are sitting at the nearby table. They look uncomfortably back at me and then away towards the books they are supposed to be reading.

What's the problem ... what happened first, in the beginning?

Finally Selina is pushed back in time – to one hour earlier when the children were first beginning to gather in front of the school.

Teresa 'wanted to do what she wanted to do'.

In other words, not what Jennifer wanted her to do?

Yes. So Jennifer told everyone that Teresa doesn't have friends anymore. And that's that?

Silence.

By then, most of the girls in the classroom are listening and all eyes turn toward me.

But I do not have an answer.

Journal entry, January 2000

Jennifer was a student in my Grade 1 class. She was lively, sociable, and almost always in the company of Selina and Teresa who, like Jennifer, were Spanish–English bilinguals. Much of Jennifer's time and interest was devoted to social affairs – arranging who would sit where, read what, play with whom and so on. During the first part of the year I was frustrated by frequent discord in the threesome and, at times, various other girls from the class. While I seldom heard or saw anything happen, feelings were hurt, tears were shed, names were called and individuals were excluded. Time and time again, Jennifer was identified as the source of such troubles – 'Jennifer says she isn't ___'s friend, Jennifer won't let ___ sit here, Jennifer told the other kids not to play with ___.' In addition to Jennifer's apparent use of language to exercise power over her classmates, the fact that she frequently did so

Continued

in Spanish (a language I do not speak) made it even harder for me to figure out what was going on.

My own writing and classroom observations provided a base for gathering data to begin to answer some of my questions. The Teaching Assistant assigned to two of my special needs students provided information normally not available to me, such as recess and lunch playground observations, comments made by students not intended for my ears, and the general impressions of another adult familiar with and to the students. The richest data came in the form of three video tapes, produced by Linda Hof, the video ethnographer member of the Teacher Action Research Group, who visited my classroom once a month during the spring. The tapes were painstakingly transcribed by me and shared with my colleagues in the group. Each taped session lasted from 60 to 90 minutes and focused on Jennifer as she and her classmates completed an assigned activity. The tasks were typical of classroom practice. They were open-ended and students were allowed a wide range of response. There was no expectation of formal evaluation; the usual procedure was for products to be shared with, and appreciated by, the whole group at the end of the activity period. Students were accustomed to sharing materials and space. As the spring progressed, the combination of teaching, watching, transcribing, discussing and writing led to new understandings and new questions – a time of rich professional growth for me. The following describes some of my learning based on analysis of the videotape data.

Video 1: Tearing Clouds – Tear paper to make a cloud that looks like something else. Complete the sentence frame, 'It looked like a ___ but it wasn't a ___.' Follow-up to reading *It Looked Like Spilt Mile* (Shaw, 1947). When I first saw Video I, my immediate reaction was 'Wow! So *that's* what goes on!' Watching what happened frame-by-frame in a place far from the classroom, I was able to see things that I never had seen. I was impressed by how little interest Jennifer showed in her own work and how much more attention she paid to Selina. But I was most impressed by the way she treated Selina and Theresa. Jennifer appeared to be a very powerful girl who actively and constantly dominated those around her. She told them where they could and couldn't sit. She pit one against the other. She hit them. She threatened to tell the teacher that they had done things they hadn't done. The notes that I produced as a result of transcribing the tape were full

Continued

of big questions – Does this go on *all* the time? With *everyone*? Where does she get such power? Is it 'okay' for this type of thing to be happening? What classroom practices affect it? Should I be doing things differently? When teachers say we are trying to help children develop 'powerful voices', is *this* what we want? None of these questions had any obvious answers and my research group encouraged me to collect more data.

Video 2: Building Towers – Make a tall tower with toothpicks and modeling clay. Draw and write about your tower. I was interested to see what effect group composition would have on Jennifer's behavior, so in the second video 'Building Towers' I placed her at a table with Selina and two other classmates – Elizabeth, a very confident girl of English background, and Andy, a younger, much less confident Punjabi-speaking boy. Jennifer reacted differently to her three table mates. As before, she divided her attention primarily between her own and Selina's affairs. With Selina, Jennifer was teasing and provocative (e.g. sticking her with a toothpick), exclusive (giggling with each other and speaking Spanish) and competitive (making sure that her tower was not shorter than Selina's). At the same time, however, Jennifer was aware of Elizabeth and Andy. Elizabeth worked very independently and interacted little with the others. At one point she asked the group in general how to spell a word. Jennifer offered immediate assistance. On another occasion, Jennifer spontaneously offered Elizabeth some extra clay, despite the fact that clay had become a scarce commodity. Andy spoke frequently during the activity, but Jennifer ignored him. Even when he addressed her directly several times, the only time she spoke to him was to tell him to stop talking.

This was a more complex view of Jennifer. Apparently she was not always the same. She had different and very distinct ways of relating to different classmates. I was also impressed by how quickly and effectively Jennifer switched from one response to another. One 50 second long excerpt showed four distinct different positions into which Jennifer moved easily and naturally. The positioning seemed to be relative to what was happening and with whom, and designed to keep her in a favorable place.

Video 3: Creating Trolls – With the people in your group, use a large sheet of cardboard and other materials in the classroom to make a Troll. My growing understanding of Jennifer's identity as multiple in nature was supported considerably by 'Creating Trolls'. In this case,

Continued

when the group was to produce a single product, Jennifer's attention was not fixed on her own or Selina's work. From the beginning, Jennifer was very excited to be grouped with Elizabeth on the project, and, during the hour or more during which the group worked on the troll, Jennifer was primarily aware of, and deferential to, Elizabeth. She looked for material that she thought would please Elizabeth. She complemented Elizabeth and gave in to her on all decisions. On several occasions she was critical of Andy's work, but when Elizabeth defended Andy, Jennifer backed away quickly.

When I viewed Video 1 I thought I had uncovered Jennifer – that I had intuited correctly. She *was* controlling and she *was* mean. It was tempting to focus on how to control or redirect that meanness and how to protect Selina and Teresa from it. But in Video 2 Jennifer demonstrated that she could also be helpful and that sometimes she subordinated herself to others. I could also see that Selina's relationship with Jennifer was not simply one of victim to tormentor. They enjoyed several moments of shared intimacy. Video 3 left no doubt that Jennifer was capable of a complex range of behaviors. As I continued to review the video taped data, it became apparent to me that Jennifer's behavior was different in different contexts, and that she used a variety of strategies to secure desirable positions for herself in her interactions with her classmates. Jennifer was not always the same. She had remarkably different and distinct relationships with a wide variety of classmates. Further, she was able to successfully manage several relationships at the same time.

Over the months of this project, my understanding changed, and with that change came a more relaxed stance toward Jennifer. Now when I look at Jennifer, I am less likely to see her as a 'problem' and am more likely to be aware of other aspects of her presence. I am more open to her, less 'on guard' against possible competition. When difficulties arise, I am more interested in looking at the context and asking myself how it might be changed in order to affect power imbalances positively, than I am in how to 'stop' Jennifer. The change in my view began with the recognition that something was not right, followed by the willingness to examine deeply. The investigation that followed was supported by my TARG colleagues and made possible by the use of video-taped data. The latter was what made it possible to move a real-life classroom situation out of the classroom to a place where I was no longer responsible for taking immediate action and thus able to look and watch and think and consider.

Continued

An excerpt from my journal in May:

At the end of Morning Circle I handed each child in the circle a piece from a brand new floor puzzle titled 'The City'. It was a spontaneous activity, but my general idea was to build the concept of 'city' and provide experience with puzzling strategies – building the frame first, looking for unfinished words such as BANK, SCHOOL, CITY HALL – as we put the puzzle together in the middle of the circle. The kids, however, were too excited to pay much attention to me, and very soon the circle deteriorated into smaller groups trying to fit together their pieces. I sat back to watch how it all happened. As they tried various solutions, many kids lost track of their original pieces. The small groups that had formed out of those sitting near each other, passed pieces between themselves and then merged with other small groups to put their sections together. In a short while, the puzzle was just about finished. At that point, I realized that I had inadvertently retained two of the pieces and had put them beside me on my bench. When all of the children's pieces had been placed, I contributed the two that had been put aside. The kids excitedly placed them, and we all sat back to admire the completed puzzle. Except – there was still one piece missing. Then, Jennifer's hand came from behind her back. She leaned forward and placed the last piece. Later, when I asked her if that was the original piece I had given her, I wasn't very surprised when she nodded 'yes'.

Seeing Jennifer as a girl who is relatively effective and efficient in negotiating her position in the classroom community of practice. I can empathize with her as she deals with the challenges that face her and can admire her resourcefulness, flexibility and resiliency. By the time Jennifer produced the last piece of the puzzle, I was ready to enjoy a quiet smile to myself. What she had done seemed an extremely clever, non-hurtful way to position herself very powerfully in relation to the entire class, including me.

The story of Jennifer emphasizes two factors as contributing to the change of Corey's attitude towards a problematic student. One was Corey's growing understanding of the multiple nature of identity. Implicit in the training teachers receive in observing children, has been the assumption that people have innate and fixed characteristics. We tend to lean on this assumption in order to explain the failure of certain children to thrive in our classrooms, and in that way it has provided us comfort. However, understanding that students' identities are not cast in stone but are different under different circumstances, actually offers great power to classroom teachers. Instead of the disrespectful, damaging and usually hopeless task of trying to fix or change our students, we can look to our own practices for change. We can seek contexts in which our students are able to show themselves differently.

The literary theorist Mikhail Bakhtin (1984) wrote about the heroes of Dostoevsky's novels as being portrayed as 'acutely sens[ing] their inner unfinalizability, their capacity to overgrow, as it were, from within and to render untrue any externalizing or finalizing definitions of them. As long as a person is alive he lives by the fact that he is not yet finalized, that he has not yet uttered his final word' (Bakhtin, 1984: 251–252). Our students are of course unfinalized, as are we, and as are classroom practices. Everything can change and be different from what it now is.

The other important element in allowing Corey to 'see' Jennifer differently, was the use of video, and engagement in classroom research. It was when she was able to closely observe Jennifer outside of the confines of classroom space and time that she discovered that Jennifer responded variously to different circumstances. Finding opportunities to observe our students engaged in activities they are competent in seems a very important activity for which many teachers have little time. Observing competence was an activity important to Suzanne Rowbotham, another TARG member.

Suzanne worked for many years as a specialist in a program for children who were identified as having social and emotional problems serious enough to be removed from their neighborhood schools. Like Surjeet, Jennifer and Raminder, Suzanne's student Tim had managed to acquire an increasingly problematic identity as he progressed through elementary school. In the following paper written for a course, Suzanne argues, in fact, that given the choice of two formal labels, Tim opted for the one that he considered to be less degrading – that of behavior problem. Fortunately, a different classroom environment provided the opportunity for Tim to be a different kind of student.

What Child Is This?

Suzanne Rowbotham

> *There have been easier worlds in which to be either*
> *a student or an educator.*
> (Varenne & McDermott, 1999: xi)

When Tim first walked up the stairs of the school to kindergarten holding his mother's hand, he was a little boy – a brother, a son, a tree

---

Continued

climber, an animal lover, a storyteller, an expert in many things. As he entered the classroom door, he became something different. He became a student. This new identity, historically and culturally prepared for him, would forever change him from being just a little boy. He would now be carefully studied and watched so that any deviance from the expectations of the normal five-year-old could be documented and analyzed.

In his early days in kindergarten, Tim displayed curiosity about the world and enthusiasm for learning in many ways. He actively participated in class discussions by contributing his personal experiences. He was confident and articulate when sharing his knowledge of the world around him. He enjoyed interacting with the other children and seemed particularly aware of the activities and discussions occurring around the classroom. Tim was seen by his teacher as a friendly and cooperative student with a positive attitude toward school. But the teacher also noted that Tim had difficulty sticking to tasks, and she felt a need to frequently redirect this attention to his 'own work'. This was seen at once as a deviation from the norm, something that needed remediation. On his very first kindergarten report card was a clear message. There was a need for this child 'to limit his socializing as it is interfering with the completion of his school tasks'.

> *The child's delay (had been) noticed. It (was) noticed by another human being, but not just any human being in a neutral setting. It (was) noticed by a teacher (not a janitor), in a school (and not at home), during class time (and not on the playground). Suddenly the difference between performance and the teacher's expectations has been made into a difference that can make a difference in the biography of the child.* (Varenne & McDermott, 1999: 5)

By the end of the kindergarten year, Tim was already being identified as a child who did not put enough effort into his work. He was lagging behind on his letter recognition and printing and was not staying focused. His kindergarten teacher recommended on his report card that Tim be reminded by parents that his behavior would influence his success at school. In any other area of Tim's life, his interest in others, his need to move around, his disinterest in the task at hand would probably been seen just as isolated fluid reactions to the world around him. It is only in the classroom that an identity is imposed and a red light goes off for all to notice. This child could have (or be) a 'problem'!

Continued

Over the next four years Tim's identity as an unwilling learner and a behavior problem became accepted and reinforced by the school community and then by Tim himself. Evidence continued to be collected and meetings regularly held to discuss the latest episodes and to support and encourage the unfortunate teacher who had to deal with Tim's attitudes in the classroom. Tim was actually becoming the identity assigned to him. Exceptions to his expected behaviors were dismissed as flukes or were completely ignored. Regardless of often contrary evidence, an assigned identity is nearly impossible to destroy.

Once a deviance has been noticed, it becomes the task of the school to collect data, make observations and analyze every deviation from the norm. The goal of the school is to attach a name to the child's assigned identity. Then it will be possible to plan for remediation. For Tim, it became a bit complicated, as labels of Attention Deficit Hyperactivity Disorder, Learning Disabled and Conduct Disorder were investigated. In the initial School-Based Team discussions, Tim was identified as a child who would not work and who was lagging behind his peers. As Tim's 'behaviors' escalated, the focus on his learning disability lessened. Teachers tried to assess and remediate the behavior that was most unpleasant to adults. By the time Tim was in Grade 3, he was refusing to do any work at all. He was reported to be in constant conflict with his teachers and was acting out aggressively on the playground. Behavior plans were developed and consequences for inappropriate behavior were clearly set out. Tim wore a pathway to the principal's office as he constantly crossed the line and teachers expressed their frustrations with his lack of progress.

As Tim was about to enter Grade 4, formal testing was scheduled. Tim willingly worked with the school psychologist. The results on many of the tests amazed those who had worked with him. Tests placed Tim in the superior range in intellectual abilities. It is most interesting to note, though, that he refused to even attempt the tests that evaluated written output, the area that had given him trouble since those early days in kindergarten. I wondered if Tim was aware that completing these test would have provided the percentage difference required to designate him as Learning Disabled, or in his eyes, Dummy. The test results remained inconclusive. Tim had beaten the system – resisting the degradation associated with the label of Learning Disabled. Instead, he seemed resigned to accept the expectations and consequences of Behavior Disorder.

Continued

Tim was placed in a Social Development program and his behaviors escalated even more. He lost all his playground time and was constantly supervised by an adult. Privileges were taken away, and he still spent much of his time sitting in the office. Tim ended his Grade 4 year angry, frustrated, full of thoughts of death and unable to trust the people whose job it was to guide his educational journey.

A new look

When Tim was assigned to my Grade 5 classroom, I decided it was time to take a new look at him and his situation. It was apparent that the school had experienced little success in getting Tim to change to meet the expectations of the school. Perhaps we needed instead to work on changing the attitudes and practices of the community in which Tim spent his time. Indeed, things finally did begin to shift for Tim when he became part of my classroom which was based on the 'community of learners' model described by Barbara Rogoff *et al.* (2001). This model (as opposed to the traditional teacher-centered instructional model) develops from the understanding that people learn best when they are taking active and varying roles in their working community. It sees children learning best when they are learning about things that interest them and when they are using their expertise to support their peers. The philosophy of the classroom is that learning is a social activity and participation by all members of the community happens all of the time. In a classroom in which this approach is taken, there are not periods of time in which cooperative and collaborative work is encouraged and then put away when the period is over. The members have a belief that collaboration and cooperation are how learning occurs. Children are never left to struggle through a task alone. There is always opportunity for members to work together and thereby be able to achieve what would be impossible to do alone.

One of the important differences I wanted to make in Tim's new classroom was to give him the opportunity to challenge the identities that had been assigned to him during his school years. One example that illustrates the possibilities that arose for Tim as a member of his new community of learners was our study of owls. After reading the novel *Owls in the Family* (Mowat, 1996), I arranged a visit from a volunteer at the Wildlife Refuge. She brought live owls and provided the opportunity to examine and dissect owl pellets. During her presentation Tim was attentive and confident. The questions he raised

Continued

were sophisticated and elicited the respect of the volunteer and his classmates. He was quickly identified as someone who *knew*. During the dissection of the owl pellets, Tim was consulted whenever a bone needed identification. He was the one who removed the living maggot from the owl pellet and bravely disposed of it. The class, as a group, decided to take their owl studies one step further and create posters that would communicate their knowledge of owls to other children. Tim immediately became immersed in the project and worked straight through lunch. He painstakingly printed out everything he knew and then began to search for additional information in books. When he became stuck on a word, he happily approached a reading expert for assistance. What had happened to that defiant, uncooperative and unmotivated boy? He took his unfinished project home and, according to his delighted mother, kept sneaking his light on to work just a little bit more!

Changes come slowly. For many years Tim had been seen as a very specific kind of student, a 'problem'. That identity was created by the community of which he was a member, and it was supported and reinforced by all members. As he continues through school, it will not be an easy task for Tim to resist what has become such a big part of his world. Experiences of the past have made him unsure about the possibilities that exist for him in his learning. Patterns of behavior that have supported his assigned identity have also limited his access to his peers and the resources of the classroom. The community which was a part of the creation and maintenance of Tim's assigned identity, now needs to take an active role in supporting him as he explores different identities – as he appropriates different language and behaviors. Only when Tim actively participates in the learning of the classroom and school communities will he begin to access all the resources that he needs.

For Tim, and for all our children, we must try very hard to examine the institutionalized practices of our schools. We must question our desires to rank and grade, to pass and fail, to force these vibrant and multifaceted beings into slots and categories. We must carefully examine the consequences of our decisions. Our educational system can be different.

We need to look for that little boy who so many years ago climbed the stairs with his mom – the brother, the son, the tree climber, the animal expert, the storyteller. Just a little boy of multiple talents, skills, interests and challenges eagerly facing his first day of school.

Raminder's, Surjeet's, Jennifer's and Tim's unfinished stories are but a few of the living puzzles that continued to draw our thinking into the complexities of human identity and to convince us that we, as teachers, are extremely influential in determining what 'kind of students' the children placed in our care become. They remind us that we need to look critically at school and classroom practices in order to avoid those that force students into defensive positions, and that we must actively challenge and resist the equation of *difference* with *problem*. We know that some children are advantaged and others disadvantaged by the decisions made about what is important school knowledge, what language that knowledge should be represented in, what modalities are legitimate for representing knowledge, and how we assess whether individual children have acquired that knowledge. We know that, disproportionately, the poor, the 'different' and linguistically and culturally minoritized children are the usual embodiers of 'failure' in representing school knowledge. TARG members came to see that these children being assigned failure identities was a result of certain school practices.

Of course, classroom teachers are not by themselves able to effect the enormous social changes that would be required to make schools places where all children can be successful. Those changes are, among other things, political and economic, and happen in arenas bigger than classrooms. But teachers are not helpless in their local circumstances. Understanding that identities are neither fixed nor unchangeable, we know that we must develop variable environments and activities that permit us all to try on many identities. Such environments (communities) and practices are often not what we are accustomed to in school, and we need therefore to look at other models, to help us create what we all need.[3] In Chapter 4, we examine more directly the characteristics of school communities and practices we find in our everyday experiences.

Chapter 4
Community and Community Practices

Ashif

Corey Denos

Early one morning as I made my way down the hall to my class-room, I was approached by another teacher. 'I want to ask a favor. I'm going to the Primary Music Festival this morning with my class, and several of my kids can't go. It's being held in a church; maybe that's why. Can Ashif stay in your room for the morning?' Continuing, 'Do you want me to send anything for him to do? Let's see. Actually, he can't do *anything*. He spends most of his time with the ESL teacher, but she's going to the Festival too. So let's see. I know, do you have a listening post? He'll listen. Just put him at the listening post – he'll be fine. He really can't do anything else.'

All of the primary classrooms at my school begin their day with Noisy Reading – 15 or so minutes spent with books. It's an informal, sociable time often joined by parents, grandparents and younger siblings. That morning there was a new face for Noisy Reading – actually two new faces because Ashif's older sister came in with him – and the two of them bent very quietly over a large story book at a table in the corner of the room. When it was time for Gathering, I took out my guitar and began singing 'Oh we ain't got a barrel of money, maybe we're ragged and funny, but we'll travel along, singing a song, side by side.' Before long all of the children had put their books away and were sitting on the carpet, some with their arms around each other's shoulders swaying and joining in on 'side by side'. I searched the faces for Ashif. He was there. Someone suggested singing 'Oh a Hunting We Will Go', a current favorite in which the kids make up the verses. Following the first chorus, a sea of waving hands was ready

Continued

with suggestions: we'll catch a little mouse and put it in a house, we'll catch a little snake and make it eat some cake, we'll catch a little girl and give her a pearl … and then from Ashif, we'll catch a goat and put it in a boat … After the guitar had been put away, Ashif's lips moved along with others as we counted the days we'd been to school that year – getting close to 100. Then we counted the days by 5s and 10s and 2s. Someone suggested by 6s and we tried that. During the previous month we had found and read and discussed more than 10 versions of Little Red Riding Hood. Over time we had retold the basic story using dialogue only and printing the characters' lines on chart paper strips. It was a long and messy process, and every so often we would divide into groups, pick a character and read through the story so far. Ashif chose to read the Wolf's lines, and he assumed a great growling voice. We always end Gathering by taking Class Temperature. We sit in a circle and someone asks each person how s/he is feeling that day. By the time Ashif was asked, he had figured out an appropriate response: 'I'm a 10 because I'm happy.'

At Choosing Time, Ashif wandered around the room for a few minutes and then joined a small group of boys who had set up a series of roads on the floor and with small plastic figures were pretending that dinosaurs were attacking the city. As the game progressed I began to hear his voice along with the others: 'Watch out! Here they come! Eek! …'. As the children went out the door for recess, I took Ashif aside and said, 'When the bell rings, come in this door. But all the doors look the same from the outside, so if you forget you can just go back in your usual way and we'll find each other.' 'Oh, if I make a mistake, I'll just go to the office', he responded with comfort and confidence. I said, 'Good for you!'

As it happened, Ashif returned with no problem and we settled in for Writing Practice. Along with everyone else, he chose a place to work and a writing book to work in. Like everyone else he came up with an idea and wrote about it. When some children shared their writing, he chose not to but listened to the others. While the regular members of the class worked on assigned math jobs, Ashif explored the math center and chose an activity that reviewed addition and subtraction facts to 10 and then to 20. Then before we knew it, the morning was over, the Music Festival attendees had returned and it was time for lunch. Ashif had spent a busy and productive morning – so busy and productive that I had forgotten all about the listening post.

In this story Corey told us at a TARG meeting, we are presented with two different classrooms and what seems like two different Ashifs. In the first classroom, community practices are organized such that Ashif is seen as someone who 'can't do anything'. In the second, he is indistinguishable from the other class members – a 'regular' kid/participant. The lesson that we all have different ways of being in different places is one that occurred over and over in our TARG discussions. As teachers, we decided that we needed to pay close attention to the *places* in which our students spend their time in school – our classroom *communities* and the *practices* or activities in which they engage there.

TARG's interest in community and practices came first from Kelleen's book, *LEaS*, in which she uses the notion of *community of practice* to theorize about classrooms. Jean Lave and Etienne Wenger (1991) proposed the notion of community of practice to highlight the social nature of learning. Looking at several different sorts of apprenticeships, they noted that to become a full member of a community of practice, one needs to have access to a wide range of ongoing activity, oldtimers and other members of the community; and, to information, resources and opportunities for participation. For Lave and Wenger, to learn means to practice with others, using particular community tools. If participation is key to learning, it becomes important that all individuals within our classroom communities are able to participate, using community tools, as Ashif was able to participate in Corey's classroom. Like Lave and Wenger, we do not think everyone participates in the same ways in particular communities; as adults in the TARG learning community, we knew that our circumstances were different and that our participation in this group could not be identical across members. We knew that some of us would learn classroom research practices faster than others; that some would learn how to present their research in varieties of ways at different rates from others, and that some of us would have to stay relatively peripheral to the research activities of the group. The group was active over time and our circumstances changed over this time. Sometimes, some of us had the time to write papers, for example, and others did not. Yet we knew that hearing the voices of each of our members was important to us and made our collective and individual work better. Was there a way to take the model of this adult learning community to classrooms, to allow children differential participation in activities that permitted differential skill, commitment and resources? Could children, regardless of difference, be included in classroom life?

As we have already mentioned, one of our earliest experiences as a group was to read and discuss *You Can't Say You Can't Play* by Vivian Paley.

Paley has written many books reflecting on her teaching practice, and her work resonated with the kinds of practices we were discussing weekly. Her guideline for creating an inclusive classroom, captured in the title, *You Can't Say You Can't Play*, was often referred to as the group discussed issues of inclusion and exclusion. For some of us involved in classroom teaching, Paley's ideas about changing school to fit children, rather than changing children to fit school, represented a shift in our thinking. Instead of emphasizing our responsibility to fix or normalize or acculturate every one of the diverse individuals who populate our classrooms, we realized that we could instead focus on developing classroom communities and community practices that make a wide range of participation possible – that would include rather than exclude that diversity. But to do so, we needed to think long and hard about innovative practices, as the classrooms that many of us are accustomed to are not focused on inclusion of diversity.

When confronted with the diversity of the classroom, the emphasis in much of our professional training was to learn how to assess the individual needs of our students – to sort them into program categories such as 'at risk', 'slow learner', 'ESL' and so on. After diagnosis, then our job was to help them learn the skills necessary to participate in the regular classroom. We try to teach them English, provide extra help in academic areas, recommend medical investigation of those unable to sit still for long periods of time, and organize social groups to help children make friends. We buy program materials for children and take in-service education workshops to help with developing 'social responsibility' and with combating bullying. When those things failed to work – or when the job became overwhelming – we sought the services of a growing number of specialists within our schools. In recent years in Canadian public schools at least, it has become relatively easy to send children out for special services. There are many places to send them – Learning Assistance Center, Social Development Class, English as a Second Language teacher, Speech and Hearing Pathologist, Counselor, Reading Specialist, Enrichment Teacher – and of course the Office, the Hall and the Time Out Chair.

In our pursuit of more inclusive classroom communities, TARG teachers wondered what difference it might make if the rules for participation in classrooms were changed. We wondered if standard practices that lead to exclusion and make different sorts of participation difficult could be challenged, and if our definitions of classroom community could be extended. The three stories that follow represent these ideas. While they concern a teacher's responsibility for fostering community, one deals specifically with the relationship between a teacher and her students, another about a student and his class, and the third with the relationship between a teacher and the families of her students. 'Learning to Breathe', presentation notes written by Sonia Sandhu, tells of her changing classroom practices to make things better not only for her students, but also for her. Suzanne Rowbotham's 'Jake – One Child's Story' tells of a classroom community that realized that participation in it did not have to be uniform. Susie Sandhu's story 'The Grandma', describes how she worked to widen participation in her classroom community, by including her students' families.

Sonia was a relatively new teacher whose research project during the first year of TARG was to examine how changes in her practice – in this case, cooperative group work – might open possibilities for herself and her students. She hoped that it could interrupt school's usual display of deficiencies, freeing students from deficit labels and allowing more equitable participation in learning for all. Sonia had had a variety of teaching experiences, but that year was working with her first full-time, year-long teaching assignment – a Grade 2/3 class. Like other classrooms in her area, Sonia's contained a high percentage of students designated as requiring special services – English as a Second Language, Mild Intellectually Handicapped and so forth. Her school was undergoing an accreditation process, and her administrator was adamant about keeping up with the extra paper work associated with children with ESL and other designations. Sonia felt obliged to follow the rules and expectations set out for her by tradition and by the bureaucratic requirements of her school and district. She felt responsible for delivering the prescribed curriculum for both grades. She spent hours on paper work documenting how she was meeting the special needs of her students. As she struggled to deal with the many challenges, she brought her trials and errors and successes to TARG meetings. One of her early concerns involved the physical organization of her classroom. She began the year, as she felt she was expected to, with her students sitting alone in assigned seats. Midway through the year, however, Sonia tried different kinds of grouping and asked tough questions about the influence of seating arrangement on student production and energy.

> I put them in groups of two for a while, but now I've changed my seating arrangement back to the original form (alone). When they were in small groups, they became cliquey and started forming little clubs. Now they're all facing each other again in a big circle. I've been punishing them. I said 'no group work, no nothing'. But they just sit there and produce nothing. The club formation is slowly fading – at least

superficially. But given any opportunity they squeeze their way to go work with a friend ... and then they produce so much more. Maybe it's the expectation I created by saying, 'You're allowed to do group work.' And now I'm saying 'You're in trouble.' ... It's just so difficult ...

A week later, Sonia reported that she had tried grouping her students in cooperative, mixed-gender groups.

I get a little panicky. They're so noisy and I wonder if they are really on task. I also see other teachers looking at my classroom. But at the end they produce such wonderful work. I do not know what's going on, but as long as they're on task I feel fine and I feel safe too.

During the months that followed, Sonia used video and audiotape to observe her students closely. She changed not only the physical organization of her classroom, but also the nature of her assignments and her expectations of product. In doing so, she found she was better able to facilitate the participation of her highly diverse class, as she reports in these presentation notes.

Learning to Breathe

Sonia Sandhu

The week before school began, I received a phone call from the District office informing me that I had been assigned a Grade 2/3 position at an inner city school. It was my own teaching job – and a huge challenge. As the year began, I was aware of the expectations of the Provincial curriculum for Grades 2 and 3. I also knew that I had additional responsibilities, mandated by the district, to my many 'special' students. I felt extremely anxious about meeting everyone's individual needs and overwhelmed by record keeping. In the attempt to keep the situation under control, I became rigid in my expectations of outcomes and learning behaviors. My students sat by themselves and worked on the isolated skills I understood to be required. And I worried about the noise level – would my colleagues think I did not have good classroom management?

But my endless planning and discipline and worrying was not working. The assignments were either too easy or too difficult. Some students required extra teaching, whereas some did not require any pre-teaching. Regardless of how long I planned, some students

---

Continued

finished early and some never did. My students seemed unmotivated, complained of boredom, and were irritated by my constant nagging about completing the assignments within the narrow expectations I had written for them on the chalk board. I was miserable. I hated the complicated arrangements within my class. I felt that I was actually damaging my students. My actions were not consistent with my beliefs and values. When I thought about the tone that existed in my classroom, I experienced such stress that I felt I was suffocating.

Finally, I reached some kind of breaking point. I realized that with all of that worrying and individualizing and record-keeping and rule-making, I had forgotten to breathe. I decided to let go for a few days – to take a rest. I tried not to think much about the curriculum, the auditors, other teachers' opinions, being the 'perfect' teacher. I decided we weren't going to do any work that required formal teaching, pre-defined expectations or closed assignments. Instead, students would work together on open-ended projects. I took away the schedule of the day and most of the classroom rules. The children could speak and engage with whomever they wished. They could move around and take breaks whenever they felt them necessary. They could drink and eat when they were hungry and thirsty. The date did not have to be on the left margin and underlined with a ruler. They could work alone or with a friend. They could use whatever materials they wished, including my own. The job I set for myself was to listen to my students and do everything I could to support their (not my) goals. And to breathe.

The difference was wonderful. For the first time I enjoyed my classroom. The students were actively and enthusiastically involved. As the year progressed, my lessons became shorter and shorter and the children assumed increasing responsibility for directing their own learning. I found that in open-ended and cooperative language learning activities, children's labeled 'deficiencies' seemed to be less apparent, while opportunities for appropriating not only language but also positive identities as successful learners were increased. More equitable and fluid social relations began to replace the traditional ranking within school hierarchies. I sensed that all of my students – even those seen as disadvantaged – had a voice and felt heard. And when they were being heard, they became more secure and more willing to try.

In the spring I observed a constellation of activities that came to represent for me the changes that had occurred in my classroom. One day I read the class a children's book about different kinds of

Continued

communities. A few days later, I noticed three of my students Aman, Albert and Jasmeet working busily on the floor and Linda Hof, our videoethnographer was able to videotape this. The children had taped four pieces of chart paper together to make one gigantic working sheet and were drawing a map of their ideal neighborhood – with basketball courts, Pokémon arcades, houses and hockey arenas. It was clear from their conversation that the activity was connected to the book we had read together, although the idea was entirely their own.

Watching them work, an observer from outside would not have known that, all three boys had been designated English as a Second Language in need of support, and that one of them was performing more than two years below expectations for his age. In this self-initiated activity, their cooperative interactions created an opportunity for all three to take the teacher lesson, add to it their own local knowledge and develop new meanings on their own. They seemed to slide out from under the labels that had assigned them to the margins. After a while other children began observing their busy work, and, in response to interested questions, the three boys proudly described the pictures on their map. Additional groups formed and began drawing maps of their ideal neighborhoods. As enthusiasm grew, I joined one group and drew the beginning of a legend on the side of their map. While the children completed the legend on their own, I was asked by others what we were doing. 'Ask them', I said, indicating the group I had just worked with. 'They can show you.'

My classroom was changing – becoming an easier place for both my students and me. I was happy to see it as a place where differences could exist but did not need to be attended to in ways that singled out some for degradation. I was no longer suffocating under the weight of my own and other's expectations. We were all taking huge breaths.

Sonia's growing realization that the decisions she made regarding grouping, noise level, assignments and so on – the *practices* she used – had a profound effect on the behavior of her students, was but one of many examples discussed throughout our meetings. Her decisions about practice also had a major effect on her as a teacher and as a person at school. School became a place where it was possible for her students to explore learning in whatever ways were comfortable for them. Sonia was able to observe her students, get to know them better and in so doing, create a better social and academic environment in her classroom. When TARG made presentations to student teachers, Sonia's description of the myriad tasks and decisions and pressures on new teachers seemed to resonate especially strongly with them. Sonia's attention to how she felt in her community, what its practices were to doing to her and her students, and the opportunity to observe, reobserve and analyze the videotape with other TARG members, gave Sonia a sense of how classroom practices might become more educative. With the support of her own research, as well as that of TARG, Sonia was able to resist her initial feelings of strangulation and of needing to do what she thought was expected of her.

Suzanne Rowbotham talked sometimes at TARG meetings about how she also felt somewhat alienated from what 'school' expected. She noted that the students in her specialist pullout program for children with social and emotional problems were also alienated when they were pulled out of their regular classrooms and that they frequently were unable, even after intensive intervention, to reclaim their positions in their classroom communities. Despite the progress they had made, they continued to be excluded. She realized that these children's successes in the educational system were not merely dependent on their attitudes and efforts, but at least as much on the attitudes and efforts of their classroom community. She decided to re-enter the regular classroom and try to create a learning community that would actively and willingly support and include all of its members. The question she asked is 'What can I do to find some way of keeping this child in the classroom? How can I make the community meet the needs of this child?' The following course paper describes her reflections on working with Jake, and how she learned to orchestrate classroom practices to better meet his needs.

Jake: One Child's Story

Suzanne Rowbotham

A simple and rather traditional assignment is given to my 24 Grade 4s and 5s: 'In groups, choose your favorite part of the novel and present it to the class in the form of a short play.' The children chatter and gradually disperse into small huddles around the classroom. Within minutes, Jake approaches me with the radiant smile saved for particularly wonderful ideas. He asks, 'Can we use props for our play?' My positive response brings forth a widening grin. 'I have

Continued

a great idea' he says, 'and I think I have all the stuff I need to build it!' As Jake flies back to his group, I wonder, as always, what he will come up with this time.

Three days later I hear the familiar sound of Jake's two-wheeled dolly rumbling down the hall. After a quick morning greeting, he sets right to work, rummaging through the material he has brought and connecting plastic tubing, hoses and boxes. He continues through Attendance, through Calendar Time and nearly all of the way through Math. Although the 'teacher' in me cries out to stop him and force his mind onto the pressing task of multiplying decimal numbers, my curiosity and wonder at his abilities keeps me silent. Soon it is time to begin the presentations of the plays. Jake begs for his group to go first, and I must admit that my curiosity is fixed most on the tarp-covered heap in the corner of the room. With much encouragement and astonished looks from his classmates, Jake uncovers a fully functioning water fountain. He has built it so that the main character in the play is able to realistically sip from a water fountain as described in the book. Once again, Jake has creatively and enthusiastically found a way to use his talents to secure a place in his community.

Jake is a 10-year-old boy who sometimes seems to be turning 50. While his classmates bring in the latest Beanie Babies or proudly display their soccer trophies for Show and Tell, Jake is liable to present a multimedia presentation on the workings of a laptop computer, complete with demonstrations of how he has adapted it for his particular needs. With great exuberance, he talks about his treasures, draws intricate diagrams of their inner working, and patiently explains everything all over again when he looks over the confused, though impressed, faces of his classmates. But he is not just a showman. Jake can be counted on to fix any computer in the lab that is being temperamental. He will eagerly search out non-functioning pieces of equipment to repair or take home to use in a new invention. Every minute of every day Jake is making plans in his head and on paper. When we began a unit on money in Math, Jake brought in a fully functioning cash register with a laser scanner that he had put together with spare parts he'd purchased for five dollars at his favorite second-hand computer store. When we began our study of weather and talked about measuring the velocity of the wind, Jake gleefully took on the project of building a wind detector so that we could take accurate measurements – and then added a remote control feature so that we didn't need to leave the classroom to read the display.

Continued

Jake was pleased to tell me that, because this was considered by his parents to be a school project, he had been allowed to putter at home with the project for over five hours – until it was working to his satisfaction.

Once I asked Jake where he got his ideas and why he spent so much time building his inventions. He told me that he is always looking for ways to make things better or easier in the world. Each day brought opportunities for Jake to look for a problem that needed solving. Because of his expert knowledge and skill level, he discovered problems of which most of us were unaware. Frustrated by a typical little boy's problem of forgetting to turn on his nightlight before getting into bed, Jake drew up plans to install a nightlight that operated by remote control. At his day care center, he built a strobe light to hook up to the recreation building's stereo system. It was battery operated and required him to transport his Dad's large battery back and forth each day. That problem was quickly solved when he turned the stool he used to reach the bathroom sink into a wagon for hauling purposes. Down the street he would merrily trudge with his little wagon, large battery and strobe light!

It would seem that school would be the perfect place for this curious, motivated and persistent child. But this has not been the case. From Jake's perspective, school has tried to take him down a road he is unwilling to follow, and there have been disastrous results. As a student in our school system, Jake has often been seen as a very difficult child.

Long before school life began for Jake, he had been identified by his parents as a child who was fascinated with the world. His mom began keeping a journal when he was very small, documenting the problems he pondered and the inventions he created. He was given an old computer at the age of five, really just a piece of junk. Unwilling to wait for assistance from his father, he was able to turn it into a functioning word processor. Already seen by his parents as a child who was very curious, articulate and possibly gifted, they had high expectations for his education. He was enrolled in the French Immersion Kindergarten program in a suburban elementary school.

On his Kindergarten report card, Jake was described by his teacher as a child who spoke 'freely at Show and Tell – this is obviously a special moment for him. He speaks with excellent English and sounds like an enthusiastic teacher!' As the year progressed, however, the comments on his report card began to reflect some conflict and behavioral concerns. 'He has the odd day when he needs to sit apart from

Continued

the others, but it never seems to bother him ...' By June, a 'behavior report book' was being sent home regularly, and there were complaints of 'rudeness to the teacher and to others, refusal to cooperate and disruptiveness during teaching time and work time'. Recommendations were made to have his behavior closely monitored by his Grade 1 teacher when he returned from the summer break the following September.

His teacher in Grade 1 felt that 'he [would] gain self-confidence and pride by doing the tasks and work asked of him instead of doing what he wants to do, the way he wants to do it .... ' Further, his 'negative attitude is affecting everybody in the classroom and it is affecting himself'. Concerns continued to be raised by his classroom teachers throughout his primary years. They included: difficulty with peers, emotional withdrawal, temper tantrums, communication difficulties and social dysfunction. It was noted in a referral for testing that 'he does not take positive feedback or positive reinforcement well. If anything it should be avoided'.

The picture of this bright and inquisitive child certainly darkened over his years at school. There was little reference to his delightful smile that brightens a room when a project has been successfully completed. There was no recognition of Jake's own special interests, his talents and curiosities. Teachers saw instead a lack of motivation, a negative attitude and an unwillingness to cooperate. Jake wasn't responding to the usual school experiences as other children do. Somehow he needed to change.

Psychometric testing done at school clarified and highlighted Jake's many strengths: his ability to express himself articulately, his understanding of his own feelings, his creative abilities in Fine Arts, his enjoyment of sciences and experiments, and his inquisitiveness. With all of these abilities, talents and interests, however, it was disheartening for all to see how very unhappy and frustrated with his educational experiences he continued to be. The system was not working for Jake.

When Jake entered my Grade 4/5 class, I wondered how we could possibly turn things around for this capable and creative young boy. I already believed that in order for children to experience significant achievement, they must be a part of a classroom community that supports and encourages the exploration of diverse and unique ideas, one that celebrates the curiosities of all our children. I felt that what was most important for Jake was that he be given the opportunity to

Continued

continue his search for problems to solve, to make plans for future inventions and to dream the colorful dreams of a 10-year-old boy. I felt that this was certainly something that could be accomplished in our schools – that we must somehow find ways of building new roads where the acquisition of knowledge and skills *and* the innovative and unexplored ideas of the child can travel hand in hand. How could I build a new educational road on which Jake – with all his energy, passion and determination – and I – with my prescribed learning outcomes and units of study – could travel on together encountering a limited number of potholes?

Making connections: Building relationships

In the early days of the school year I experienced many of the frustrations expressed in the recorded accounts of Jake's school history. Each new activity, regardless of how interesting or exciting it seemed to the rest of the class, was greeted with Jake's rolled eyes, looks of distaste and expressions of fatigue and boredom.

My instinct told me that initially it was important for me to establish a relationship with Jake. I needed to find out what really excited him and what he really wanted to learn. I schedule interviews with all my students early in the year so my curiosities about each of my new students can be satisfied. During long and animated conversations, I quickly discovered what excited Jake – electronics and inventions. His face lit up and his body came to life as he discussed the latest piece of equipment he had salvaged from the pawn shop. Jake clearly articulated that he felt he learned best by reading, by asking questions, by thinking and by working with his hands. He called himself 'a hands-on kind of guy', and I realized it was important, when developing a learning plan for him, that these preferences were taken into account. An important component of developing a trusting relationship was listening to Jake. It seemed to make sense to make sure that he was involved in his own educational goal setting.

I also needed to learn about the challenges he faced. Before addressing this issue, I felt it important to share my own passions and challenges. After hearing about my phobia concerning technology, Jake willingly confided his challenges – his frustration with writing, his confusion in many areas of math and his uncertainties with physical activities. As Jake and I shared ourselves, an important relationship

Continued

began to form. I also connected with Jake's parents, and we talked together at great length about their frustration with Jake's school experiences and their concern that he did not easily fit into the social world of 10-year-olds.

In addition to learning about the individuals in my classroom during the first months of the school year, I focus on building a supportive and caring classroom community. We make particular efforts to explore the skills and interests of our members so that we are able to make use of our resident experts throughout the year. Jake was quickly identified as a child whose special talents and knowledge would be of great benefit to all of us. As Jake began to see himself as a respected member of our classroom, many of the negative attitudes and behaviors started to fade. He began to shine in response to our earnestly sought advice on a variety of topics. In addition to serving as our computer expert, the props that he created for class plays and the instruments he contributed to science studies made learning more exciting for everyone. Every eye turned to the door when we heard Jake rumbling down the hall in anticipation of what he would share next.

Finding a balance

During a great majority of Jake's formal education, his time in the school system, he fought against the authorities who insisted that he would be much happier and more confident if he developed the skills and knowledge deemed important by the school. Jake strongly believed that many of the skills insisted upon by the teachers were irrelevant to his personal goals and interests. Many of the negative behaviors that were reported related to his insistence that he didn't need to learn 'all this stuff'. It was nearly impossible for Jake to show any interest in anything that was outside his realm of expertise. As mature as Jake was in many areas, however, I also believed he needed to increase his reading and writing fluency and develop mathematics skills. This was the first huge pothole in the road. The more adults tried to convince him of the importance of these skills, the more Jake resisted.

There needed to be a balance in Jake's school life. I decided that my task was to help Jake understand the importance of specific skills and knowledge in the development of his wonderful ideas and inventions, feeling that if he did so, he would be more motivated. I decided to approach this in a cooperative and negotiable manner. By collecting

Continued

information from a variety of sources, Jake was able to see the relevance of many school skills. For my part, if Jake was willing to make a serious effort to work on those skills, I would allow great flexibility in how that work could look. Jake decided that he would do most of his written work on a laptop computer that he had salvaged from the pawn shop. He donated a printer he had rebuilt to the classroom so that his assignments could be handed in on completion. Most of Jake's project presentations are done using multimedia technology. Over time we've worked out an arrangement whereby Jake does three hours of homework every night. Basically, he does his schoolwork at home, and he does other things (such as computer maintenance) at school.

As time has gone by, Jake has had the opportunity to contract his services out to desperate staff members with dysfunctional equipment. Jake knows that as long as he completes all his assignments he is welcome to help out in the school. He is now seen as a respected expert in the school community. With the added responsibility and recognition, Jake is willing to take more risks in his learning. As confidence builds, he is becoming more involved in a variety of classroom and school activities, and he is seen by his classmates as a wonderful and knowledgeable friend.

I often question the risks that I take, moving my students away from practices that are so familiar and down a different, often uncharted, road. Am I merely being an 'easy' teacher, giving in to the whims of demanding and indulged children? By encouraging children to become active builders of their own educational paths, am I setting them up for failure in more traditional classrooms? When I listen to the comments of my colleagues, when I proudly watch Jake receive school awards for citizenship and school service, when I see him being given the responsibility of maintaining the computer lab, when I see him joking around with friends on the playground, I have to believe that our year together had positive effects on the whole school community, and especially on Jake and me. My hope is that by giving Jake the freedom to explore his world in his unique way and finding ways to feel satisfaction in his school world, we are creating the opportunity for another great inventor to make a difference in our world.

Both Sonia and Suzanne's stories point out how community practices affect educators as much as students. School practices make teachers, as much as students, feel rated, judged. Many teachers ask: Am I an 'easy'

teacher? Do I have 'proper' classroom control? Are my students too
noisy? Such questions may be especially troubling to teachers with less
experience. However, Kincheloe (2003) sees such insecurities as affecting
all teachers regardless of their experience. He argues that current practices within educational institutions are based on 'western industrial
organization with its bureaucratic, hierarchical structure' and practices.
Teachers are taught to be '"supervisable", to be team players, to fit into
organizational structures' (Kincheloe, 2003: 2). With a mania for 'accountability', curricula are 'so specific in their prescribed list of "facts" to be
covered that the best teachers are handcuffed in their efforts to teach complex concepts and to connect them to the lived experiences of students'
(Kincheloe, 2003: 4). It is interesting that Sonia describes a feeling of strangulation and Kincheloe calls it being 'handcuffed'. Finding the courage to
take action, to make the kinds of adaptations that Sonia and Suzanne
demonstrate in their stories about their classrooms, cannot be easy, but it
is brave work.

In her story about Jake, Suzanne reminds us that taking different paths
is not without stress. The questions she asks regarding risks she might be
taking, her own motivations, and the unknown future are tough to deal
with. There is a great deal of pressure – from ourselves, other teachers,
parents, administrators, the 'system' – to do things the way they always
have been done and the way 'everyone' does them. Many of us get the
sense that we 'see' things differently and find ourselves making choices
that are different from those of our colleagues and advisors. It is easy to
feel alone, and it was widely recognized that one of the strong motivations
for attending TARG meetings was the support we found there. Anxiety
about the effects of our decisions arose frequently during TARG discussions, and as we searched for ways to make our classroom communities
more supportive, we realized that TARG was becoming just such a community for us. We all spoke at one time or another about the significant
personal strength we received from our participation in a group where
we encouraged each other to explore our worlds in our 'unique ways'.

As group members began to discuss their first research topics, Susie
Sandhu, an experienced teacher in a school enrolling many immigrant
students, turned to an area of special interest to her and told us:

> I'd like to focus on parental involvement. I think that's so important.
> I've started with parents coming in and reading with my Grade 3 stu-
> dents in the morning for about 15 minutes. Everyone is very busy, so
> I've had only a few parents drop by and, I do not want to put them
> under pressure. Right now they mostly sit and listen to their own

child – just getting comfortable. Some of them do not even take their jackets off yet. I'm working on that.

When Susie talks about her classroom, she usually talks about families. While much research and most teachers agree that a close connection between school and home is advantageous to students and their families, Susie's most commonly stated reason for encouraging parent participation is, 'They (families) are the children's first teachers, and as an educator I need to learn more from them.' The degree of respect implied in that statement, is illustrated in many ways. Susie always positions herself as a learner, and she is always careful not to push her teachers, her students' families. 'They are all so busy ... working shifts and more than one job. So whenever they have time – just getting them in the door, making them feel welcome and involved and let them know that they are so important.' She understands how difficult coming into the classroom can be and patiently waits for parents to feel comfortable enough to 'take their jackets off'. 'I had a breakthrough last week with the mom who only reads to her own child. I turned around and there she was reading with my "most ESL" student. She'd moved her chair over by his desk and there she was. Those kinds of things, you know, just make such a difference.' In Susie's classroom there are few barriers to participation. You can be a dad, mom, grandparent, younger sibling, or any other friend or family member. You do not have to speak English or be able to read. She has in her classroom bilingual children's books in the languages of her students and families, and Susie makes it clear that she think reading in all languages is highly valuable. 'Two of the parents are unable to read in their first language, so I have a variety of wordless picture books available.' In Susie's classroom, you are always welcomed gratefully and respectfully. The presentation notes that follow provides not only a portrait of Susie's classroom, but also an example of how her policy of inclusion has affected the rest of her larger school community.

The Grandma

Susie Sandhu

It was a fall day when Surinder's Dad arrived early to drop off her permission slip for our neighborhood walking trips. He was always the one who delivered Surinder's school fees, signed forms and other

---

Continued

school documents. She is the youngest of his four children and he liked to take special care of her. He and I chatted about allowing Surinder to take on the responsibility for returning her own school papers. But while I wanted to encourage her independence, I did not want to discourage Surinder's Dad's participation. I told him that we start our mornings with a short reading program in which family members are invited to stay and listen to the children read. 'My English is not so good. I can't read English, and I can't read Punjabi very well' he replied. I switched to Punjabi right away and stressed that all parents are most welcome at any time in our classroom. They are the children's first teachers, and as an educator I need to learn more from them. I showed him the dual language books we have in our classroom. Surinder told her Dad that she could read an English book to him and then tell him about the story in Punjabi. So he came in and sat at the little round table. Soon he was repeating the sentences Surinder was reading and greeting her classmates. When it was time to go, he came over and shook my hand. He seemed a little hesitant and asked, *'Jaruri hai?'* – *is it necessary?* Do I really have to come? 'Just when you have time', I answered, because I know he works long hours and spends a lot of time with his children. 'Whenever you can, just for a few minutes' and explained to him how important it is for his child. So he came – twice the first week and three times the next. His confidence grew, and he began conversing with other English-speaking adults and children in our classroom. Surinder was so proud to have her dad at school. She said one Monday morning, 'I wish I could come to school everyday. I do not like weekends'.

Like many of my students, I am the child of immigrant parents. My Dad was literate in English and Punjabi, but because girls did not attend the village schools during her childhood in India, my Mom never learned to read or write. That did not stop her, however, from coming regularly to Open House afternoons at my small Vancouver Island school. She sat for long periods at my desk, poring over my notebooks and reports, and though she couldn't read or understand the words, she must have found important meanings there. The attention she paid to my school life was certainly meaningful to me. Her regular presence, positive comments and interested questions inspired all of her children to work hard at school and helped me decide to become a teacher.

Continued

For more than 10 years I have taught in an urban school that includes Kindergarten to Grade 4. Out of our total enrollment of 270 students, approximately 90% speak English as a second language. The majority speak Punjabi. Other home languages include Bengali, Cantonese, Gujarati, Hindi, Swahili, Tagalog, Spanish, Tamil, Urdu and Vietnamese. Almost all of my students' parents work full-time outside the home. Many do shift work and many have more than one job. They work in restaurants, hotels, banks, airports, hospitals and nursing homes. They work for construction companies and as taxi drivers. The majority of my parents are learning about the Canadian school system along with their children. I know from my experience in the Punjabi community that many of these parents were educated in a much more teacher-directed and structured system. Many are uncomfortable in our less formal classrooms. In their own school experience, teachers were considered to be experts, to be left alone to do their work without interference from parents. In addition, many of the parents of my students do not speak English fluently and find it difficult to communicate with teachers. For these reasons, many of them hesitate to step through the classroom doorway. My fluency in Punjabi has been a great asset in reaching out to many parents. I also depend on my students, colleagues, and other parents to help as interpreters. I make an effort to learn a few key phrases in all of the languages of my students.

After beginning the day with the reading program, we usually go for a power walk around the perimeter of the school. The quick jump start really makes a difference for all of us. Besides fresh air and exercise, it gives us an opportunity to chat with each other. Parents who have been reading with us often come too, and as we walk along the sidewalks, other extended family members sometimes join in. Over time we have become familiar with many different people in our community. One man, who lives next door to one of my students, used to be quite unpleasant. For years he muttered remarks as we passed. He was unfriendly and frequently complained about things going on at the school. When we wished him a good morning, he just looked at us. But during the past couple of years he's changed. He began to respond with a smile or a 'Good Morning' in return. Now there's a bit of conversation. Many of my students' caregivers are their grandparents, and I've noticed that many of them, after delivering their charges to

Continued

school, enjoy staying around for a while and visiting with one another. So we often stop and chat with groups of grandmas during our power walks. They have taught us how to exchange morning greetings in many different languages. One day while power walking I stopped and chatted with a grandma, and when we moved on she thanked me for taking the time to talk to her. I do not know who her grandchildren were, but she seemed really lonely and often smiled when she saw us coming. A group of Chinese grandmas frequently stay and do Tai Chi on the playground behind the school. Another group of Punjabi grandmothers remain a while and stand together chatting – often with preschoolers playing around their legs. As we became familiar with each other during the crisp fall mornings, I suggested to the Punjabi grandmas that they join the Tai Chi group. They were quite hesitant, saying that they could not communicate with them, but during a later power walk, I noticed them trying a few of the exercises from a distance.

Grandma S, as the students came to call her, was in her late 80s when she became part of our classroom community. Her daughter and son-in-law left for their jobs early in the morning, and she was the caregiver for their four young children, two in school and two still at home. She was already a favorite with some of the teachers because of her bright smile and frequent warm hugs. When she began coming to our morning reading sessions, she apologized for her lack of English. 'I speak Punjabi. I'm too old to learn English. Let the kids learn it; it's too late for me.' But I told her, 'We have so much to learn from you and we want you here. The children will learn so much about respect and culture.' Grandma S especially liked the dual language books. She usually sat at a small table with several children, including her grandchild, and read them stories in Punjabi. She developed such a nice relationship with the students, and they taught her how to write her name and then how to write the numbers to 20. After that, we got her a little notebook to keep track of her new words. The children showed her how to write her address and phone number – you know, survival English. Once I watched Grandma S listening to a child read. After a while she said, 'OK, now it's my turn' and started reading from her scribbler. She was reading the numbers. After the morning power walk, Grandma S often stayed on a while in the classroom. She would settle into the rocking chair with one of her preschool

Continued

grandchildren. The children would show her their work, chat about community or school activities and teach her how to say words in English. She said, 'I like to see that they are all working hard and learning, but I think I am learning from them too!'

One Friday I stayed home with a cold. When I came back to school on Monday, I was met at the door by Christina, the university student who volunteers in my room. By the time I got to my classroom, the story Christina told me had been repeated by two other teachers. Apparently, when I was away on Friday our sweet little Grandma S had come in and was sitting there with her little journal and her pre-schooler granddaughter. The Teacher On Call (TOC), who had been sent to substitute for me, took Christina out in the hallway and said, 'I feel very uncomfortable with her (Grandma S) here. Would you go down to the office and get someone to remove her from the class-room?' Poor Christina. That was only the third time she had been to the school! But she said to the TOC, 'I don't think she's bothering any-one and I don't feel comfortable going to the office.' Then the ESL teacher came by and when Christina told her what the problem was, the ESL teacher talked the substitute into letting Grandma S stay. But somehow word got around because the children came to me and said 'Mrs Sandhu, on Friday we heard that Grandma S was leaving and we made a thank you card for her. And we wrote her notes.' Apparently even the gym teacher knew all about it. She told me that she had seen the children's notes. It was some incident! I think just about every staff member came in on Monday. I didn't get too much done. I feel so happy that the rest of the school had come to value Grandma S as much as I did. I am grateful that they stuck up for her.

The way Susie schedules her day, the role she plays during the daily reading program and power walk, and the material she uses, are choices she has made based on the value she places on family involvement, liter-acy, physical exercise and more. 'Practice' is what we *do* as teachers – how we ask questions, how we organize and present ideas and information, how we respond to students, how we provide opportunity for practice. We are accustomed to thinking of teaching practice in relation to student performance in subject areas. When we are attracted to new ways of doing, we are looking for more effective, efficient, accessible, interesting ways of getting students to read better, add faster or more accurately, or …. But we have come to see that teaching practice is not only about reading programs and science textbooks (although those are involved in practice). We believe that practices are what a community does, and classroom communities do much more than learning to read, or conducting science experiments. As we saw with the work we did in our previous chapter, we believe that classroom practices create who children can *be*, and that has profound effects on what they can learn.

TARG members had any number of examples of school practices that they believed did not contribute to the development of healthy democratic communities. One teacher spoke about the newly instituted practice at her school of giving slips of paper to the recess and noontime supervisors of the children. These slips of paper were to be handed out when children were observed misbehaving – something like traffic tickets. If any particular child accumulated too many of these slips, they were summoned to the principal for punishment. The TARG teachers felt this practice encouraged school adults to look for misbehavior, instead of looking for cooperation, competence and initiative. Another teacher spoke of a decision in her school to have 'silent lunch', so as to ease the responsibilities of the supervisors. Again, TARG members wondered if setting up such a difficult-to-follow rule made misbehavior inevitable.

One of the most hopeful books about education we have seen recently is edited by Barbara Rogoff, Carolyn Goodman Turkanis and Leslee Bartlett (2001), *Learning Together: Children and Adults in a School Community*. In it, the editors open with a description of a school in which they participated: 'an innovative public school that prioritizes *instruction that builds on children's interests in a collaborative way, where learning activities are planned by children as well as adults, and where parents and teachers not only foster children's learning but also learn from their involvement with the children* (Rogoff *et al.*, 2001: 3, their emphasis). Beginning with the argument that schools today are modeled on factories [processing 'the raw material (the children) in standard ways prescribed by experts for the workers (the teachers) to carry out' (Rogoff *et al.*, 2001: 6)], Rogoff *et al.* (2001) described the school with which they were involved as a 'community of learners' in which both adults and children have varying responsibilities to foster children's learning. The school, which has been operating for over 20 years, engages parents in participation in the learning community, and involves them in teaching and learning along with the children. As we noted above for TARG, varied ways of community participation are expected and valued in this school. The book contains chapters written by parents and teachers and shows in great detail how children, teachers and parents come to understand how to be members of this community and how their participation involved them deeply in learning.

The stories we tell – of Surjeet, Ashif, Jake, Grandmas and the other members of our shared classroom, including the children in the books and articles we have read – serve to remind us that there are important choices to be made in developing our classroom communities. Teachers choose the requirements for participation. Teachers choose the scope and breadth. Teachers choose the practices. Of course, choosing is not always easy. Besides the time and energy involved in reflecting carefully upon what is going on in our classroom communities and seeking alternatives, there can be significant resistance to change. But we must keep reminding ourselves that we *can* choose and we must practice making choices. We have to actively seek out alternatives to the ways things have always been done. We have to resist pressure to maintain the status quo. If we want to be able to say that our classrooms are inclusive – that they support the growth of all members – we must accept our responsibility to be aware of the choices to be made and to be aware of the effects of those choices. The next chapter looks generally at an ubiquitous practice of schools – helping – and tries to examine what the effects of making choices about helping might be.

Chapter 5

Help

Balancing Rocks

Anne Scholefield

While working in a teacher education program at a local university, I was able to participate in a variety of professional development activities with my teacher peers. One such event was held at an outdoor recreation camp where about 60 of us attended a three day retreat. I had seen photographs from the year before, of what appeared to be sculptures made by teachers from the rocks along the shores of the river. They were beautiful images, prehistoric, elegant and graceful stones balanced on stones in what appeared to be impossible formations. The setting and the unlikeliness of the configurations lent a kind of magical, sacred feel to the sculptures. I was curious to know how they were made, but at the same time, I was pretty sure that I would never be able to make one.

So I was excited to learn that opportunity had been provided for those of us who wanted to 'explore' how these rock sculptures were built. We met on the river bank one morning. We were shown the basics of choosing rocks we could carry and how we might begin with larger rocks at the base, adding the smaller, lighter ones as the sculpture balanced and grew. The expert demonstrated how to use our hands to guide each rock to balance. After a minute or so, he balanced one stone on another, end on end. His sculpture, like most of the others, quickly became taller than it was wide, and a figure-like silhouette began to emerge. I found a space on a granite boulder above the river. The sound of the rushing water discouraged conversation, so we worked without talking, stationed intermittently along the bank. I found a couple of stones weighing about 20 pounds each, and took them to the boulder I was using as a base. When I had placed the

Continued

72

first stone, I lifted the second and placed it on its point, or tip, so that, rather than lying horizontally across, it rose vertically from the stone below. I was mimicking the other sculptures I had seen, not really believing that I could balance such a heavy, asymmetrical rock, but, having seen the other sculptures, willing to try.

The memory includes the feel of the warm sun on my back, the fragrances of the forest and river, and the pouring sound of the water rolling to the sea. Kingfishers were flying and diving and squawking, and scraps of conversation floated by like driftwood on the river. The rock perched unsteadily between my hands and swayed left and right, back and forth, as I repeatedly coaxed it to assume a fixed position where I had imagined it should rest. Time passed. My legs grew uncomfortable as I squatted. My mind became reassured that I had been right to believe I wouldn't be able to do this. I relaxed and quit trying to guide the stone to its place of equilibrium. Instead, I began to attend to beauty of the surroundings. Within moments, the stones spoke a quiet, confident click. The rock stopped moving.

Slowly, slowly, I moved my hands away from the rock I had been trying to control. I sat back and waited for it to tumble off and clatter down the bank. However, the stone had taken a seat and was not about to move without some prodding. I was surprised and pleased. I could be a sculptor after all.

The process with the third rock and the fourth rock was the same. And so too, with the second and third sculptures. The sooner I stopped trying to control the stones, the more quickly they were able to find their own balance, their place to stand. Each time I gently tried to coax them to where I thought their equilibrium would establish itself, the balance and 'click' never came.

It seemed a little corny, but I came away from that exercise with a renewed awareness of how as a teacher, I am so often disposed to help and in so doing, assert my will, my intentions on students who have an educational path that they need to assert for themselves. A kind of humility is required, I think, to be able to allow the students to work with the circumstances we teachers set up, so that the students can create and experience their own 'clicks', to generate and to produce their own learning. Once I had organized the conditions for the sculpture to happen, I had to allow the stones to do the rest. Any other act was interference. It wasn't me who balanced the rocks. The rocks balanced the rocks.

Surely one of the most commonly-held motivations behind teachers' work is the sincere desire to help. While teachers may take different stances on what is important to learn in school, on exactly what best prepares children for their futures, and what constitutes the most effective methods and materials, we are not likely to be found among the passive bystanders of our world. We are involved and active. We want our students to be successful. We have a commitment to the future. We want to make a difference, to make things better. We have chosen to belong to one of the 'helping professions'. TARG members, of course, are no exception. The desire to be more effective helpers (both of individuals and of society in general) is something we all hold in common, and sometimes the frustrations we shared during meetings focused on our inability to help enough. As Bonnie Waterstone put it in her dissertation about TARG, '... we shared a common interest in improving conditions for those traditionally marginalized, in particular classroom practices that fostered the inclusion and participation of everyone' (Waterstone, 2003: 18).

Although we subsequently realized that several of us were already working on various aspects of help, it was Colleen Tsoukalas who first focused the group's attention on 'help' as a topic of special interest. Colleen's long career as a teacher has been devoted to providing some of the extra assistance required by teachers who are unable to meet all of the needs of their highly diverse classrooms. She is one of many specially trained teachers hired by school districts to provide support to teachers in a wide range of areas – English as a Second Language, Special Education, Speech and Hearing and so on. So in a sense, Colleen is a helper of helpers – a specialist/itinerant/helping/resource/learning support teacher – and her varied experiences over a long career have provided her with a unique perspective in our discussions. During the years of our TARG meetings, Colleen moved from one helping position to another and frequently expressed frustration with the difficulties she found in establishing helping relationships with the many children and teachers in her care. 'You know that there are so many kids out there who need support. You're the resource teacher, the one they turn to. So how do you get in and make it happen – or at least try? You can't just sit out in the hallway.' One afternoon Colleen arrived at our TARG meeting excitedly waving an article titled *Beyond Benevolence: Friendship and the Politics of Help* by Emma Van der Klift and Norman Kunc (1994). She said that the ideas presented in the article had helped her to look at her classrooms and schools in new ways. During the many rich discussions that followed Colleen's contribution, we found that the ways in which help is handled in classrooms can have complex and profound effects on identity and community.

Helping others is considered something to be encouraged in growing children. Buddy programs, peer tutoring, cooperative learning groups and so on, are widely used in today's schools. However, Van der Flift and Kunc took issue with the assumption that encouraging children to help each other will lead to inclusion. They made a distinction between a *helper–helpee relationship* and a *reciprocal friendship*.

> We must guard against merely creating another generation of 'professionals' and 'clients', with the former group seen as perpetually competent and the latter, perpetually needy. Unless help is reciprocal, the inherent inequity between 'helper' and 'helpee' will contaminate the authenticity of a relationship … In most societies today, helping others is viewed as a socially admirable course of action. Those of us who are in a so-called 'privileged position' are asked to give to others. We know we should give to our families, our communities, and most of all, to those 'less fortunate' than ourselves. Yet, why is it that most of us, while perfectly comfortable offering help, are decidedly uncomfortable receiving it? … the problem lies primarily with the lack of self-determination commonly experienced by 'helpees'. It seems that often dignity must be forfeited in order to receive help. The power to decide where and when help should take place, who should help us, and whether in fact help is needed is stripped away. (Van der Klift & Kunc, 1994: passim)

The stories that follow are about helping in schools. First, Joanne Thompson writes about two children assigned to a helper–helpee relationship by their teacher – a relationship Joanne later wrote about in her Master's thesis. Thanks to the use of video and the services of a translator, her research offers a rare glimpse of the difficulties we can unwittingly create for our students. Kelleen Toohey's and Natalia Gajdamaschko's presentation notes examine 'help' in two classroom communities. Taken together, these pieces provide paradoxical advice to teachers – a reflection of the complexity of help we are beginning to appreciate.

Jan and Chelsea

Joanne Thompson

Words such as 'share' and 'help' are often used as teachers work with their students encouraging them to be 'good community members' and creating positive and supportive learning environments.

Continued

My thesis research focused on the notion of help, specifically the common practice of buddying up one student to help another. I studied how this assigned relationship affected language learning and identity. The focus students were two Grade 4 Korean girls. Chelsea had been in Canada for one year and had been asked to be a 'buddy' or 'helper' to Jan, who had just arrived from Korea. The teacher had instructed Chelsea to 'teach Jan about school and Canada'. With the assistance of Linda Hof (TARG video ethnographer) and a Korean translator, I was able to focus on how this assigned relationship, that is, identifying one girl as helper or expert and the other as less knowledgeable, affected the interaction between the girls, the girls and the rest of the class and the girls and their teacher.

As I read through my research data, particularly transcripts of the girls' interactions that had been translated from Korean, I began to question if the notion of help is as warm and fuzzy or as static as we teachers hope it to be. I was also reminded of how sophisticated students are at masking their dialogue.

The following dialogue is from a translated transcript dated a month into the buddy relationship. The two girls were asked to sit at a table separate from the class. Chelsea, the old timer, had been asked to help Jan, the newcomer, with her math. Throughout the interaction, both girls appeared to be diligently working on the assigned task and speaking in Korean. Prior to this dialogue, neither girl had shown any interest in the research camera or videotaping procedures.

The videotape of this interaction showed two girls, with their heads down working on a math assignment. However, the accompanying translated dialogue revealed Jan, the newcomer, to be distressed over the teacher underestimating her mathematical abilities as well as about her assessment of Canadian students. It also revealed her inability to change the situation or negotiate a more favorable position. Chelsea, on the other hand, showed how much she had invested in being the 'more knowledgeable' student, and was very adept at using the idea of surveillance (e.g. 'the camera is watching you'), increasing task demands and her knowledge of classroom protocol to maintain her position as helper.

Teacher (in English):   Chelsea, help Jan understand how to carry the one's to the ten's to the hundred's column.

Continued

**The following is a translation of Jan and Chelsea's conversation which was spoken in Korean.

Jan: I should do this math with you. I will tell you.

Chelsea: No. I should tell you about this.

Jan: You'll teach me? But it is so easy.

Chelsea: Yes, that's what the teacher said.

Jan: I already know how to solve them!

Chelsea: No, in English.

Jan: In English?

Chelsea: You can solve it in this way …

Jan: No, not that way. I'm teaching you now.

Chelsea: And put your name on the paper. Is it easy? There is one, what is the name of one in English?

Jan: I know! I know! Should we do this together? Teacher thinks I don't know how to.

Chelsea: But sometimes you didn't understand what she said.

Jan: Then did she mean that you should tell me what I didn't understand?

Chelsea: And you have to memorize this – you should know how to spell it.

Jan: Then I will ask the teacher.

Chelsea: The camera is watching you, not me. And those with a sticker are not taped. [This referred to other children in the classroom who did not have permission to be videotaped and were marked with a sticker on their shoulders.]

Jan: You mean they don't need to solve these?

Chelsea: No, the camera is not watching them. Are we erasing these at the same time?

Jan: Canadian kids are not good at math. Worse than me! (finishes worksheet)

Chelsea: Why don't we put these here?

Jan: What do you mean?

Chelsea: Final … put them on this table.

This transcript is but one of many that have persuaded me to rethink the notion of help and what we are really asking of our students. I have come to believe that giving help is very complex. It creates and/or maintains identity positions and it can either enable or restrict access to information and community for both the helper and the helped.

As with many TARG stories, Joanne's growing awareness of the complexities of the standard practice of assigning buddies, was achieved by going to a 'different place' – in this case through the use of video tape, language translation and close and thoughtful observation – where she could see that which is not readily apparent. Those of us with whom Joanne shared during her ongoing experiences with Jan and Chelsea, will never be quite the same. We will continue to encourage children to help each other. We will continue to participate in formal and informal 'buddy' relationships. But we will always remember our intimate view of two little girls locked in their quiet struggle. And, we hope, we will not forget how problematic helping relationships can be. Jan and Chelsea's story reminds us of at least one other member of our shared classroom, Jennifer. While we usually do not have access to everything that is 'going on' for our students, we can remember that there are very real and very powerful and well-hidden negotiations that are affecting our students at all times. TARG discussions regarding Joanne's work with Jan and Chelsea ranged even further and raised the sticky issue of teachers' responsibility. As Joanne said, during one of our meetings,

> With Chelsea and Jan, I am looking at the evolution of a relationship. I keep thinking back to one of my early questions of their teacher: 'How did you introduce them?' Because as we begin a relationship with somebody, that first framing is just so important. Apparently with Chelsea and Jan it was quite casual. 'Chelsea, can you help out Jan? Can you be Jan's helper?' But now that Jan is surpassing Chelsea in her academics, Chelsea can't let go of her assigned responsibility and Jan doesn't know what to do with it. Also, as soon as students are paired, it's inevitable that their abilities will be compared. Because they are together, you want them to perform together, to develop a symbiotic relationship. But often times it doesn't work that way. And then, what do we, as teachers, do? Do we just walk away from that and let it evolve? What is our role, now that we've contrived that relationship? What is our role in maintaining it or dissolving it?'

As TARG members continued to look at how teachers help, we began to see that even the way we use the word can distort our intentions. 'I was only trying to help', is sometimes used by both adults and children as an excuse for doing something hurtful. Is it okay to hurt someone if you are trying to help? 'Well I *tried* to help', can be used to excuse the speaker from further responsibility. If you tried to help and the situation didn't change, is that the end of your responsibility? 'If you want my help ... listen' or 'If you want my help ... do it this way', contains the threat that failure to behave in a certain way will bring an end to the help. Does an offer to help mean the helper has the right to control the situation?

Kelleen Toohey and Natalia Gajdamaschko (2003) investigated our society's ambivalence towards 'help' in a paper published in the Vancouver Centre of Excellence for Research on Immigration and Integration in the Metropolis Working papers. This excerpt describes some of the classroom data they examined and some of the questions they raised regarding help.

Communities of Practice and Help[4]

Kelleen Toohey and Natalia Gajdamaschko

> [Vygotsky] argued that children through their acquisition and use of language come to reconstruct a social world that contains within it the experience and knowledge of prior generations. Thus children's socialization must be understood as a social and collective process, whereby children do not construct their knowledge 'in solitude' but they do it as a 'multiple voices' endeavor, in multiple communities of practice with adults and peers who share their sense of belonging to a culture. (Carugati, 1999: 226)

Vygotsky's conviction that learning is social reconstruction of culture in a variety of social configurations and activities has been critically helpful in charting new directions for second language learning research. In this paper we consider how sociohistorical theory about communities of practice and activity are helpful in understanding events in classrooms in which children are learning a second language.

Lave and Wenger's (1991) term 'community of practice' provides a way to identify social groups on the basis of participation in particular activities or practices. Defining social units on the basis of participation in activity is congruent with post-structuralist notions of shifting identities, and multiple memberships. Lave and Wenger recognize that persons are differentially situated within activity systems and that these are not systems in which all persons are participating in exactly the same actions. They also point out that learners receive social guidance as they come to participate in community activities. Bruner (1978) developed the concept of scaffolding to describe the contribution of adults or more skilled partners to children's learning. Many other researchers have subsequently used the metaphor of scaffolding

Continued

to refer to the activity engaged in when a more experienced participant performs those portions of a task beyond the competence of the less experienced participant, so that the latter can focus on those parts of the task she can perform. Some observers have debated the aptness of the metaphor to describe teaching and learning, arguing that it misleads in suggesting that newcomers or children are passive (like buildings) in the learning process and that agency is centred in the adult 'scaffolder' or constructor of the scaffolding.

Barbara Rogoff (1990, 1995) and her research team (Rogoff *et al.*, 1993) at the University of California at Santa Cruz, in their examination of the limitations of the metaphor of scaffolding, emphasize how learners or children participate actively in the joint involvements they have with others in culturally important activities in their specific locations. They look for example, at how mothers or caregivers in a variety of cultures guide the participation of children in the activities of their communities. In one particular study (Rogoff *et al.*, 1993), they examined how mothers or caregivers of North American Anglo-European descent and Mayan mothers from Mexico teach their children how to manipulate a Russian nesting doll, a novel toy to the children. These observers noted that the skills that were valued, the means of communication and the extent to which children entered into adult activity versus adults sharing children's activity, were different between the Mayan and Anglo dyads, and argued that these different means are related to the kinds of activities that are valued and necessary for adult participation in the cultural and political institutions of the two societies. For Rogoff (1990), the notion of scaffolding is too static – she doesn't see children learning things passively and then doing them, nor does she see what children learn or how they learn it as disconnected from what their society learns or values. Rather, she emphasizes that children are always participating in the activities of their communities, and their participation is guided by other children and adults at all times, in ways that are connected to ever larger contexts of social participation. Rogoff's attention to the specifics of how adults guide or help children has been fundamental in our interest in the classrooms we discuss today.

We have also found Soviet psychological research on learning activity useful for our analyses of classrooms. In Vygotskyan theory, knowledge is not in the world to be absorbed, nor is knowledge latent in our brains waiting to be awakened. Rather, it is generated and constructed by humans acting in the world. Therefore, what needs to

Continued

be examined are these acts, or *activity*, a goal-directed, tool-mediated set of coordinated actions. We are interested in this paper in examining two distinct communities of practice, two classrooms, in which children are guided by peers and teachers to internalize given societal knowledge. In addition to considering this given knowledge, we also wish to examine how learners themselves in these situations may be enabled or constrained in the development of learning initiative, or orientation toward future learning.

Site and Methodology

The site of the study to be described here is an independent school in British Columbia that serves Punjabi Sikh children from kindergarten to Grade 12. The first author was involved in a three-year ethnographic study at this school in which a group of six focal children were observed from the beginning of their kindergarten year to the end of Grade 2. Research assistants and Toohey observed in the children's classrooms once a week, audio taping children each time; also a trained video ethnographer videotaped their interactions once a month. Teachers and parents were interviewed at least twice each year.

The children who attend this school are all Punjabi Sikh and all enter school speaking Punjabi. Their experience in speaking English varies. Some children are true beginners in English with no previous experience, while others are much more experienced users. Their teachers at the school are all provincially-certified, and are predominantly Anglo-European Canadian, although there were three teachers in the school at the time of the study who were Punjabi Sikh and members of the same temple in which the school was located. The school teaches the regular British Columbia curriculum, with the addition of a half hour of Sikh studies in the temple at the beginning of the day and a half hour of Punjabi literacy classes in the afternoon. The school is located in the basement of the temple, near the temple's *langar*, or dining hall; thus, many adults, speaking primarily Punjabi, are around the school at all times.

Striking in the data we reviewed from the Punjabi Sikh school, were the variety of ways in which adults and children in classrooms guided one another's participation. Focusing on the Grade 1 and Grade 2 classrooms, we noted that there seemed to be at least four different structures of guidance available in them, and each seemed to

Continued

draw forth different kinds of social relations among participants, and thus, different sorts of language. The four structures were:

(1) Teacher asks a child to help another child with a defined school task.
(2) Children help one another without teacher direction.
(3) Teacher helps children whom she judges are having difficulties.
(4) Teacher gives help to a child based on a student request.

We present examples of each below so as to examine what kinds of social relations these interactions establish, and what kinds of language they call for.

Data

(1) Teacher asks child to guide another child

In the Grade 1 classroom, the practice of children helping other children was a very common occurrence. As in an audio taped lesson in September, the Grade 1 teacher, Mrs Sran[5] (a Punjabi Sikh woman and member of the temple) commonly instructed the children: 'You can help your neighbor, please. If you have done it, you can help someone.' In audio taped parent–teacher interviews, Mrs Sran commended several children to their parents, saying that she or he 'helped other children'. The following example is from one videotaped morning in Mrs Sran's classroom that particularly well illustrates how children guided one another's participation in classroom activities.

Upon school entry this morning, the children were instructed to work on phonics worksheets at their desks (arranged in 'pods'), and while they were doing this, Mrs Sran worked with small reading groups on the floor at the side of the room. The children working with her shared storybooks with partners and took turns reading aloud. Some children required assistance with their reading and both the teacher and other children provided this help, sometimes reading along in chorus with the reader, and sometimes supplying words or initial letter sounds. Navjeet, who had just returned from an extended trip to India, had been instructed to work individually on a 'Math booklet', and he was having difficulty completing its title page. The title page was to have text on it ('My Book About Six') and drawings of different combinations of six. He came to Mrs Sran on the floor and told her he was stuck. Mrs Sran said to him, 'You don't know how to

Continued

do that, and Dave will help you; OK, he will help you. Is it okay [that Dave will help]? *(in a louder voice, calling)* Dave, would you please help Navjeet how to do that work because he wasn't here; he was in India and he doesn't know how to do it.'

Excerpt 1

[Dave and Navjeet are side by side at a desk. Navjeet is sitting at the desk while Dave is leaning over him and explaining with the aid of his book.]

Dave:	Like look Navjeet, like this. I drew the one and five here. And how did they become six? *[looks at Navjeet]* 'Cause you count like this: one, two, three, four, five, six. Here, like that. You know?
Navjeet:	How are you supposed to do this?
Dave:	You draw one circle.
Navjeet:	Right here?
Dave:	Yeah. You do a 't' right there [to finish off the word 'about'] You draw five circles now. Are they six?
Navjeet:	No.
Dave:	If you add this one?

[Navjeet nods his head.]

Dave:	Ok, then**
Navjeet:	Write?
Dave:	And draw a six. That's how you do it, okay? Okay? You got it now?
Navjeet:	Where are we supposed to draw it in there [inside the booklet] now?
Dave:	Same thing. Draw it like this, same thing. How can you make another way of six? Okay? Two and four. Look, two and four; one, two, three, four, five, six. *[He counts on his fingers to demonstrate.]* Move your fingers.
Navjeet:	How do you do this?

[Dave opens his book to check his answers.]

Dave:	Two and four, four and two, six and none.

[Navjeet writes down the numbers and then checks them in Dave's book.]

In this excerpt, several of Dave's 'guidance' utterances ('Are they six?'; 'How can you make another way of six?' are exact replications of utterances Mrs Sran had earlier in the year and earlier that day, used to assist other children in the class. Dave clearly had appropriated

Continued

the teacher's voice and in effect, could represent in this interaction both himself and his teacher. However, we can also see that Navjeet initiates and maintains joint action with Dave by soliciting Dave's views on what he should do in this learning activity. Navjeet's participation has a product – his continued attempts to ask the questions that will aid him in finding out what he does not yet know, in order to complete the task.

After Dave leaves the table, Navjeet examines Dave's book and begins to 'help himself' or copy from it. Dave returns to his desk and sees Navjeet copying from his work. He makes no comment and after a few minutes, Dave directs Navjeet: 'OK, Navjeet, now get your journal and write about something, write about yesterday, OK?'

In the Grade 2 classroom, children helping other children with school tasks was not as common as it was in the Grade 1 classroom and in examination of approximately 30 hours of videotape, we found no examples of the teacher directing children to help other children, and only a few examples of children helping children.

(2) Children guide one another

The following excerpt recorded in the Grade 1 classroom shows an example of another common practice: children guiding children without teacher direction.

Excerpt 2
   [*Devi and Parm are sitting side by side at their desks.*]
   Devi: We need some help. [*hits her fist playfully on the table*]
   Parm: I don't. I'm going to look at this one.
   [*Devi looks at Parm's paper.*]
   Devi: I'm going to look right here.
   Parm: You are a copy-cat. Have you found it?
   Devi: I found it!
   Parm: Where?
   [*Devi shows Parm and they both smile and giggle.*]
   Parm: I found it. Here it is. I wish they would put this over here.
   [*points at paper*]
   Devi: I wish they would put the bell right here. [*points at paper*]
   Parm: [*laughing*] I wish they would put the bells on here. I wish they would put the bells on here. [*points at different objects on the table*]

Continued

In this excerpt, the children collaborate in completing their Find-A-Word assignment. This type of help was common in their Grade 1 classroom, and it was often, as the written transcript does not fully reveal, joyful and joking. 'Expertise' shifts in this example with Devi first declaring, 'We need help', and then presenting herself as providing help. A kind of reciprocity about asking for and giving help is here displayed and the girls experience joint focus on the task. They also engage in language play toward the end of the clip, play which sounds quite a lot like a traditional pattern drill. The affect they display however seems quite unlike any pattern drills we've taught to language learners!

In the Grade 2 classroom, as already mentioned, the teacher discouraged children helping other children and children were aware of this, as shown in the next excerpt from that classroom:

Excerpt 3

[*A girl and boy are leaning over a desk and speaking in soft voices. She is helping him. Another boy approaches the desk and observes what is happening*]

Boy 2:   You're not allowed to help him. [*he walks around the other side of the desk*] You're not allowed to help him.

[*The girl stops helping the boy, but she waves her hand in a dismissing way at the second boy*]

(3) Teacher guides whom she thinks needs guidance

The third kind of guidance we have identified is when a teacher provides help to a child on the basis of her judgment that the child needs help. Consider this example from the data:

Excerpt 4

[Mrs Sran is standing behind Aman's desk observing her work]

Mrs Sran: You just left the 'T'. [*she whispers to Aman*] You need to go backwards, longwards, upwards. [*she points to Aman's paper*] What you did, this one, does not fit. Like the T, N, I, the letters are the same but this is different. This one is T, I, E, N, not this, okay? [*Aman then goes on to correct her work*]

In this example, Mrs Sran corrects Aman's circling of a collection of letters. She whispers her help to begin with and then leans down and

Continued

points out the error explicitly. Aman erases her work and Mrs Sran moves away. As is often the case in classrooms, Mrs Sran must move away because she needs to survey other children's work and to be alert to others needing her help. It is not clear from this clip whether or not Aman has been helped in any permanent way, as the video-tape's gaze, like the teacher's gaze, is sporadic and incomplete. It is also not apparent that Aman produces much during this activity that is potentially helpful for any future activity. Rather than a 'learning activity', this looks more like a 'doing school' activity.

(4) Teacher guides when child requests guidance

The final kind of guidance we wish to examine is that in which a teacher responds to a child's question or request for help. In this example from the Grade 2 classroom, Mrs Bailey helps a child after he has asked her a question, while she is directing the whole group.

Excerpt 5

[*A student asks an inaudible question. Mrs Bailey is standing in front of the class with her left hand on her hip, waving her right index finger and shaking her head.*]

Mrs Bailey: Not another one of those questions, no, no, no, no, no.
Student A: What one?
[Mrs Bailey leans towards the student.]
Mrs Bailey [*whispering audibly*]: Stupid ones.
Student B: A silly question.
[*Mrs Bailey leans toward this student*]
Mrs Bailey [*whispering audibly*]: They're stupid ones.

[*She shakes her head in disapproval. She walks toward to the student who has the question, while quickly observing other students' work along the way. She stands to the side of the student with the question.*]

Mrs Bailey: Don't count the big numbers, alright? [*pointing at the student's paper.*]
Don't count the big numbers, alright? You know what the big number is, count the little numbers. Show me the little numbers.
[*Mrs Bailey moves behind the student and takes the student's hands.*]

Continued

> Show me the little numbers. Now, take this finger then point; eight
> [*Mrs Bailey takes the student's finger and points it to the page*] nine, ten, eleven,
> [*Mrs Bailey takes the student's finger and counts the numbers on the fingers of his other hand.*] That's your answer.
> [*The student writes the correct answer in his notebook.*]
> Now, show me the little number. [*Mrs Bailey takes the pencil out of the student's hand.*] Show me the little numbers on your fingers. Show me on your fingers three. [*Mrs Bailey uses the same technique as previously mentioned to count the numbers.*] Alright, now eight, nine, ten, oh, flip-flop, wow!
> [*The student writes the correct answer in his notebook.*]
> [*Mrs Bailey takes the student's hands again.*]
> Now, show me the little number. Show me the little number on your hand, five. [*Mrs Bailey repeats the same counting technique.*] Now, seven, eight, nine, ten, eleven, twelve. Good boy.

Mrs Bailey initially responds in exasperation to this child's question, but as was typical for her, she quickly goes to the child and energetically helps him continue to do his work. Again, because the teacher is responsible for helping more than only this one child, she moves away before it is entirely clear that her help has made a permanent difference in his ability to do the work. As well, in both situations of teachers guiding children illustrated here, the teacher is the 'knower' and the child has rather limited opportunities for linguistic contributions. In both cases, the teacher stands while the child sits, the teacher directs from behind and in this excerpt, the teacher even guides the body movements of the child. This is not a situation in which the child displays learning initiative beyond the initial question he produced.

Discussion

These data describe interactions in two classrooms, two distinct communities of practice. Although both are use a provincially-mandated curriculum, use many of the same learning and teaching artifacts, are located in similar rooms in the same school, are led by provincially-certified teachers, and involve the same students (albeit in two different

Continued

years), at least some practices within them are different. In the first classroom, taught by a Punjabi Sikh teacher, the activity of students guiding other students was encouraged, valued and frequently took place. In the other classroom, the similarly-credentialed Anglo teacher commonly discouraged/disallowed such peer interaction, although she was energetic in her own attempts to guide children. In this classroom, peer guidance was infrequent. These are distinctly different sites in which learning conventions, distribution of labor and interactants in some specific practices are different. While both teachers provide instructional communities that fulfill mandates of the provincial authorities, they do so in markedly different ways. Students also produce different artifacts in the different activities in which they are involved in the two sites. It is the learning artifacts children produce, in this case, learning initiative, in which we are particularly interested here.

With peer guidance, illustrated especially in the excerpt in which Dave helps Navjeet, Dave (the more experienced participant) appropriates teacher-like language to guide Navjeet. At the same time that Dave, for example, sounds like a teacher, he is *not* a teacher, and Navjeet continues to ask for assistance. His questions are not high level, but they maintain the interaction and provide Navjeet with practice in indicating his need for guidance.

It is worth recognizing that in this peer interaction, Dave knows and Navjeet does not know, but it seems that their power relations are more horizontal than a teacher–student relationship. Dave sits beside Navjeet, so even his physical positioning is similar to Navjeet's, and finally, Dave has the material resource of his own booklet that Navjeet can copy. Teachers, despite their considerable intellectual resources, do not often have such material resources to offer.

In the Devi and Parm's example, these girls assume what appear to be reciprocal relations of power, as they collaborate in finishing their task. They seemingly happily play with language. As Day (2002) observes, when child language learners 'play' with language, they can often be seen to be providing for themselves practice in speaking the second language. Also, in so doing, the children display comfort in indicating their need for help, as well as confidence in their ability to approach the task.

In the example of Mrs Sran guiding Aman and Mrs Bailey helping a student, we see another side to guidance. In these situations, the

Continued

children who are helped say almost nothing, and the teachers take all the initiative in establishing the relationship and in structuring the learning task. In such situations, it is impossible to assess whether or not the teacher's guidance has been effective, or if it answers questions the learners are asking.

We believe that when children (and perhaps especially language learners) are encouraged, even directed, by their teachers to help one another with school tasks, to guide one another, their helping practices can be much the same as their teachers' and in some cases they use the exact words of teachers' help. They appropriate aspects of the teacher's voice, to use Bakhtinian (Bakhtin, 1981) terminology. Children see and hear their teachers helping other children in a variety of ways – reading with them, telling them words, taking over aspects of the task and so on. Children's help is thus, using Bakhtinian terminology again, multi-voiced – the child uses teachers' words but those words must fit in a child's mouth, and the child's interlocutors can challenge those words in ways that might not be possible when teachers' words come out of teachers' mouths. Sometimes in such interactions, children provide help that is indeed demonstrably helpful, and as they have done the work themselves (unlike teachers) they have material resources to share that are helpful for the helpee.

In other classrooms, or perhaps at particular times in all classrooms, children are discouraged by their teachers from helping one another. At such times, the teacher is the legitimate expert, and children appear to have rather limited opportunities at such times to guide their own learning.

Rogoff *et al.* argue that

> For middle-class U.S. children, the skills and patterns of social interaction practiced in school may relate closely to those necessary for eventual participation in the economic and political institutions of their society. (Rogoff *et al.*, 1993: 233)

The practices in the two classrooms we describe here are not unusual or extraordinary in any way in Canadian classrooms in which we have observed, or in the literature describing North American classrooms generally. Having children see the teacher as the legitimate guide to participation in the classroom was seen by Waller (1961) as a time-honored schooling practice. Preparing children for the economic

Continued

and political institutions of North American society may necessitate them learning that assistance comes from recognized authorities, that 'help' is scarce, and that finishing first, or not requiring 'help', is a valorized position. Whether or not teachers wish to support these arrangements is another question.

In contrasting the two teachers, Kelleen and Natalia first remind us that practice makes a difference and then stimulate big questions about what might be better. As Kelleen put it during a TARG discussion,

> For me, the important thing is don't focus on diagnosing or fixing the kid (or even the teacher) and instead focus on the practices. Think about the practices and think about whether you want those practices in the place for which you have responsibility, or are you going to try to counter those practices with something else?

TARG members often discussed how attention to helping practices became useful in their action research on their own and others' classrooms.

TARG members also became aware of the extents to which their English language learners 'helped' their families in many and various ways, and like others (Bigdeli, 2007; Chu, 1999; Tse, 1996; Valdés, 2002) paid particular attention to the children's reports of translating and interpreting English texts for their parents. Orellana and Reynolds (2008: 51) described 'the range of texts, genres and forms that immigrant youths engage with as they translate for their families in everyday situations'. We have already described how TARG teachers and researchers searched for or tried to design school situations in which children who had problematic identities in schools could 'shine'. As the research went on, we became increasingly aware of the growing literature that examines how skills children develop outside of school might be 'leveraged' [or, as Michaels (2005: 137) put it: 'recruited as strengths', in school]. These realizations of the particular competence of ELLs in out-of-school contexts and their relative 'invisibility' to teachers was important in TARG members' growing realization of the necessity to seek opportunities to communicate with parents and families in finding ways to link school activities with home and community activities.

Like everything, it seems, 'help' is intriguingly complex. Teachers and researchers do have a hard job and big responsibilities. But our positions require us to make choices, and it is through those choices that we have the power to create new possibilities in this world.

Chapter 6
Possibilities

Unless ... keeps you from drowning in the presiding arrangements.
Shields, 2002: 149

As long as we can formulate visions, possibility persists.
Kincheloe, 2003: 2

How do we create (or re-create) new possibilities for ... the revitalization of the public sphere, and also promote decolonization of lifeworlds that have become saturated with the bureaucratic discourses, routinized practices, and institutionalized forms of social relationships that see the world only through the prism of organization and not the human and humane living of social lives.
Kemmis and McTaggart, 2005: 571–572

The pressure on public education today is extreme. It comes from all levels of government, multinational corporations, publishing companies, the media, organized religion, universities. Everywhere there are loud and very powerful voices demanding, proscribing and legislating ... not only what should be done, but how and with precisely what results. We believe, however, that much of the success of schooling rests upon individual teachers and individual kids. All of the standards and pro-grams and expectations and funding requirements in the world are not as powerful as the relationship between a teacher and her student. That is where those of us who have chosen to teach, need to look for change. It is at that level that teachers need to come to know their individual students, develop the courage to challenge inappropriate and irrelevant voices, and recruit support from others. Those of us who are not satisfied with the 'real world' – the world the way it is – and who want the world to be different, need to challenge those voices who want conformity, who want us to fix or normalize or acculturate children to meet the needs of the larger society, who look for magical programs or methods or tests or rules.

It is easy to become overwhelmed, cynical and discouraged. We need to believe that it is *possible* for things to be otherwise – for each young human being to find her own way into active and meaningful participation in the world. One of the special gifts of 'the Little Girl Who Wanted a Hug' is her ability to articulate her questions and desires and worries. In a perfectly clear voice, she says, 'I am this. I want to be part of the world. What do you think?' Like all of her classmates, she needs to feel that she is competent and agentive. She needs to have friends, and she needs the support of other human beings. But what are the possibilities for her? With a measurable intellectual handicap, coming from a people at best marginalized in our North American world and at worst despised and feared, living in a family regarded by the prevailing social institutions as abusive and dysfunctional, and being dark-skinned, poor and female – it is hard to imagine a world full of possibilities for her. But that is what we must do. It is our job to see possibilities, to build on her obvious out-of-school (and in-school) strengths. When we look over our classrooms when we begin the school year each September we need to look for those possibilities, not in fancy new programs nor a new set of higher standards nor in pull-out programs designed to reduce the number of problems we have to deal with, but in the faces before us.

One September Suzanne Rowbotham looked out over her Grade 2 classroom and saw her new assortment of eager young challenges – including a young boy named Sam. Her story, written in a different form in her Master's thesis (Rowbotham, 2003), is a testament to the importance of identity, the power of community, the kind of help teachers can provide and the existence of possibilities for us all.

Sharing Sam's Journey

Suzanne Rowbotham

> *He is strong and beautiful but fragile. I have to build a safe and secure place for him and let him know that we – the class and I – will be there for him.* (Ladson-Billings, 1994: 111)

Sam has been a student in my classroom for three of the past four years. He loves to go on the swings at recess, cuddle with our guinea pig, run around the gym and read books. He draws great pictures and goes wild with the paintbrush. His smile lights up our classroom. Sam, just like everyone else, faces challenges and struggles, and it is our responsibility as his friends to support him in any way we can. Sam has been diagnosed with Down Syndrome and autism.

Continued

In September 1999, when Sam came into my Grade 2 classroom, he already had a large and detailed Individual Education Plan and a very supportive school team dedicated to supporting him in the school by trying to address his identified needs. He had been given the support of a full-time Special Education Assistant in his first year of school, and Pippi had been working directly with him ever since. His parents were actively involved in his educational planning and his school experiences. Sam had many adults involved in his life, both in the school and in the community. I must admit I was overwhelmed on reading through his thick file.

I have spent much of my professional life working with children with significant challenges and have enjoyed my experiences with these children, their families and other professionals as we developed school plans that address their social, emotional and educational needs. I have enjoyed building personal relationships with the children, and I have felt that I was a good listener and someone whom children could trust. When I first met Sam, I did not feel the same confidence. As a seven-year-old, Sam had limited verbal language. To communicate his needs he was limited to some basic words, signs and gestures, and the trust that his caregivers would recognize his needs. I was frightened by the fact that I did not know how to communicate with my young student. Here, he would be depending on me to care for him, to teach him and to keep him safe. I was feeling very inadequate.

Over the next few days, I watched Sam, I listened to Sam and I thought about Sam. I thought about him while driving to work. I thought about him at home while I watched my own children play. I thought about him when I observed him in my classroom and out of the playground. I talked to his parents, to previous teachers, to his SEA and to other professionals. My fears turned to curiosities. How could I give Sam the best educational possibilities, the best access to the resources of the community, and the best opportunity to be an active participant in our classroom?

Watching Sam stare out of the classroom window or rock back and forth, alone in the corner of the classroom, turning away from the enthusiastic interactions of his seven-year-old peers, I realized that I did not have enough understanding about his needs and challenges to build a positive and relevant educational program for him. We needed to create a plan that would not only address his intellectual development, but also address the significant issues that are connected with autism, specifically impairments in socialization and communication.

Continued

I spoke with the knowledgeable team of experts who were involved with Sam. I recognized the profound effect that autism had, particularly on his ability to access the resources of our classroom community, to become a participating member and an active learner. Sam had developed a close relationship with Pippi, who had been working with him since he entered kindergarten. She seemed to be able to understand what Sam wanted and needed. She generally was able to work around any resistant behaviors. In the past, most of his school day had been spent working directly with Pippi. His classroom participation involved being guided through tasks with hand-over-hand direction. But when I observed Sam at work, his gaze was often just beyond the activity at hand. He seemed 'disconnected' from the rest of us. Pippi's fondness for Sam was obvious to all, and he certainly returned the feeling. It was for Pippi that Sam save his biggest belly giggles, when she cheered his accomplishments or tickled him in the tickly spot at the back of his neck.

Although he already had an extensive adult support system in place, I felt that Sam needed regular opportunities to develop meaningful relationships with his peers. I could have just left things as they were, but something really bothered me about Sam's school experiences. He was certainly cared for and kept safe at school. He was in our classroom, doing school activities, but it just did not feel like enough to me. I wondered whether any of his school experiences were really relevant or important to him. Did he feel connected to his school community and the people with whom he shared his classroom every day? In the flurry of seven-year-old activity, in a classroom that encouraged playing and working together and where helping was expected, I would watch Sam, staring out the classroom window, rocking in the comfy big chair or gazing just past our eager faces. What was he thinking? How was he feeling? Did we frighten him with our wild squeals and energetic play? I was greatly troubled by my unknowing. I also wondered how the other children felt about Sam. Did they also feel unsure of how to relate to him? Did they have questions they needed answered? Did they also want something more for Sam? Did they think 'something more' was possible? I became increasingly dissatisfied with the school experiences that we were providing Sam. Somehow we needed to travel down Sam's road, walk beside him and share experiences with him. The only way that I felt Sam could really become a part of our classroom community

Continued

and develop friendships with his peers was for us to personally share ourselves with him. I looked around my classroom at this sweet group of caring young children. I really wanted Sam to get to know us. I wanted the opportunity for all of us to share our knowledge, stories and friendships with Sam.

I realized that I would need to make use of all of the resources I had available to me so that we could meld into a productive and positive learning community. I would not be able to accomplish this alone. With my class list in hand, I counted up the support personnel that were attached to my students, the professional experts. Pippi worked with Sam for the full school day. Another student with severe behavior disorders and blindness had a part time Child Care Worker. The Speech and Language Pathologist had two of my students, as well as Sam, on her case load. We had access to the District Autism Support Team. In the best interest of all my students, I wanted to get my support personnel into the classroom.

I carefully reviewed Sam's educational plan and identified the most important aspects of the plan. Sam needed consistency with established routines. He needed to be able to have access to a visual schedule of his day so that he could know what could be expected. He needed methods to communicate with his peers. He needed to learn skills that were relevant and important to his growth and development. After this, I began to explore ways in which Sam's classmates could actively support Sam's learning. I decided that I wanted to address Sam's communication and socialization impairments by developing a buddy system – one that would allow Sam constant access to the language and interactions of his peers. Ultimately, I wanted to put him in the center of his community. I decided that this would be my focus, my contribution to Sam's life experiences.

As a result, the buddy program began to emerge and develop. I decided that I would have Sam working side by side with a buddy throughout the school day. I would rotate through the class list, so that every child would have the opportunity to work with Sam approximately every four weeks. Next to Sam's desk a special 'buddy desk' was set up. On the desk surface were a number of brightly colored stars with encouraging comments attached for the buddy's use. Inside the desk were the 'tools of the trade': wooden puzzles, special felts and a variety of activities and games that the buddy would use with Sam. There was a large pocket chart by the classroom

Continued

door that listed all the children's names with their pictures attached. Once a child had the opportunity to be Sam's buddy, their name went to the bottom of the list. It quickly became the first stop for the children in the morning on entering the classroom. Who would be Sam's buddy today?

Next, I realized that the children in the class would need specific skills and knowledge to make this program work. It would be ridiculous to expect Grade 2 students to know how to interact or work with a child with such significant challenges without some kind of formal instruction. So I invited the Speech and Language Pathologist, Mrs Adams, to come into my classroom and formally teach communication skills to the children. She explained the importance of helping Sam focus on the communicator, keeping language simple and direct, giving him wait time when requesting a response from him. She helped us understand that by using the language 'first this, then that', Sam would be able to make sense of our expectations. 'Sam, first read book…then guinea pig.' Mrs Adams worked regularly with the children for a month and then became a resource person and an enthusiastic supporter of the program. Over the year, Mrs Adams would spend time with Sam and his buddy of the day, to introduce new concepts and ideas that we could then use in the classroom. The children were given the opportunity to practice these skills with each other and with Sam. This gave the children some useable skills, not only for their interactions with Sam, but also to use in their other social relationships.

The role of the Special Education Assistant dramatically shifted as well. Instead of working alongside of, yet separate from, the other children, Sam would be immersed in the community of his peers. Pippi's role became much broader and more complex. She had the opportunity to use her creativity and talents to develop and participate in the activities of the classroom community. She had the time to better acquaint herself with all the children and then she was able to explore ways to support their developing relationships with Sam. She needed to understand their personal strengths and challenges so the activities we designed would be appropriate. The children also needed to develop their own relationships with Pippi so that she would become a person they could trust, someone to whom they would turn for help and who would listen to their concerns. So Pippi would regularly take small groups of children out of the classroom to talk about

Continued

Sam's special needs and their role as his buddy. They needed to understand that the adults would continue to be 'in charge' within the classroom. We would be there to support, instruct and guide them while they worked with Sam. Their role was to be a working buddy, a friend to Sam. This role was so significant because as adults, we could never have that kind of close peer relationship with Sam. They were extremely important to Sam because they would be able to teach Sam 'kid stuff', the things that have importance in their culture. The children also needed to learn about the specific challenges of autism and Down Syndrome. They learned how the skills they were teaching Sam related to his educational plan.

These meetings also gave the children the opportunity to explore their personal thoughts about people with special needs, their uncertainties about their relationship with Sam and their mixed emotions about taking on this new role. We hoped that the children would be able to express their concerns in a safe and nonthreatening environment. We wanted the children to ask questions and look at some of the preconceived ideas they may have generally about people with special needs and specifically about Sam. They needed clarification about what Down Syndrome and autism entailed. They needed to learn facts about these disorders and be able to process the information and fit it into their personal understandings. In the training sessions, they were allowed to openly and honestly discuss these issues.

The children also needed the opportunity to try and make sense of some of Sam's specific behaviors. Sam often engaged in repetitious behaviors such as body rocking and arm flapping. The sessions with Pippi gave them a time when they could gain the knowledge they needed to feel comfortable working with Sam. Often, it is the lack of factual information that makes people feel uncomfortable.

Over time, the children developed an understanding of when Sam needed some time to rock and when it was time to bring him back to the task at hand. It was very natural for a child to reach over a small hand and gently rub Sam's back, and for Sam to immediately respond to the reminder. Often Sam's rocking behavior increased when he was feeling overwhelmed by his environment – during school assemblies, when different people were in the classroom or if we were doing a different type of activity. Sometimes Sam was just bored or uninterested in what was happening and would get lost in his own thoughts. His friends' gentle rubs did not bring attention to the behaviors,

Continued

nor did they punish his behaviors. They let him know that his friends were aware of his discomfort and were close by.

Suggestions were also made of ways that they could include Sam into their outdoor play. By talking together they began to see that just like them, Sam had strengths and favorite activities.

We felt that, for this program to work, the students must not feel deserted. They must not be left to feel frightened or unsure of any situation that may arise. Not only must the buddies feel safe enough to continue working on this relationship, but Sam must feel safe enough to begin to connect with his buddy. Many times, especially in the early days, Sam was resistant and noncompliant. Many times the buddies felt unsure of how to react to him or understand what he was trying to tell them. At no time did we want the relationship between the buddy and Sam to be uncomfortable or unhappy. Pippi was there, close at hand to smooth any difficulties before they got out of hand. We were extremely protective of the fragile relationships that were beginning to develop. With time and patience I believed that all the children would move into a more comfortable and predictable relationship with Sam.

For many of the children, especially those who were quieter or displayed less confidence in their social interactions, Sam's buddy program was an opportunity to feel more powerful. Kate was one of the first children to be Sam's buddy and her turn also came on a day when we were video taping. With the camera pointed at her interactions with Sam, you could feel her initial discomfort. Pippi carefully positioned herself within Kate's sight and proceeded to coach her through the math activity that Sam was doing. Kate's frequent glances towards Pippi sent the message that she was feeling unsure or uncomfortable. Throughout the task, Pippi would join the work, modeling language that Kate could use with Sam and then step back. Words of encouragement could be heard off camera as Kate continued to work through the task. Kate's growing confidence became evident as she sat up taller, began to use a louder and clearer voice and smiled proudly when Sam successfully completed the task. Buddying with Sam has given Kate the opportunity to try being a different kind of girl in a safe and supportive environment. She was able to put away her shy, nonspeaking identity and try the identity of a confident expert for a while. Little moments like these reminded me that this program was not only a positive experience for Sam but for all of us.

Continued

Over the first months of the program, the children became more comfortable with the language that worked best for Sam. They confidently set up his daily schedule using a picture communication system (see description in Siegel, 2003). This system was developed to assist children with a variety of disabilities to communicate with others. In addition to his daily schedule, Sam had the next two activities of the day attached to a small chart with Velcro on his desk. The chart said 'First ... Then ...' The children quickly incorporated this language into their communications with Sam. When Sam found an activity frustrating or undesirable, reminders of 'first this job and then this activity' helped keep him on track.

Sam also had the opportunity to become the expert while working with his peers. One of his classmates, Alan, had lost his eyesight in the summer before Grade 2. This sudden loss had a devastating effect on him as he struggled to make sense of his changed world. I wondered how I could possibly expect Alan to take on the responsibility of supporting another child with such significant special needs. After a quick discussion, Pippi and I realized that we could not exclude this child from his buddy day and would have to deal with any problems as they arose. First thing in the morning as Alan and Sam worked on one of Sam's favorite wooden puzzles, the first difficult situation arose. Using his fingers to trace the shapes, Alan was unable to find the correct spot to place the puzzle piece. Over the next few minutes, Sam gradually became aware of the dilemma, took the piece from Alan's hand, then put it into the correct place. He looked over at his buddy and smiled. 'Thanks, Sam!' came the response. In our efforts to help our students, especially those with special needs, it was easy to overlook or miss opportunities when these children could feel powerful and capable. By stepping back, by our not becoming rescuers, Sam was able to reach out and become the helper.

An important component of Sam's program was 'down time', an opportunity for him to move away from the hustle and bustle of a busy primary classroom and retreat into his own space. Into his daily schedule, there were times when Sam could choose one of his preferred activities. Originally, these choices were: looking out the window, computer time or books. These activities were done within the classroom, but in isolation. Sam would become upset if anyone came near or tried to share this time with him. His gaze was steady and he seemed to be unaware of our presence. It was difficult for all

Continued

of us to 'bring Sam back' when it was time to make a transition to other class activities.

Early in the year, a parent in the school gave us two guinea pigs for class pets. These tiny creatures quickly became a vital part of Sam's program. His favorite choice activity became 'PIG'. His buddy would gently put a towel over Sam's lap and then place one of the guinea pigs down, before sitting next to Sam's chair. Together they would stroke the animal, talk to it or just sit quietly thinking their own thoughts. Sam was able to have his 'down time' but no longer was sitting alone. The guinea pigs provided a common ground. Glancing over at the two children, sensing the calmness, the distant look in both their eyes, I often wondered if these little friends had been able to visit Sam's special world and if the experience was as serene as it looked.

As a part of our daily routine, all children were assigned a 'sharing day'. This was an opportunity to bring special treasures from home, share amazing talents or tell wonderful family adventures. This important part of the day encouraged all of the children to speak from a position of power on a topic of personal expertise. As a hesitant public speaker, I feel that it is important to provide opportunities for children to address anxieties around speaking in front of an audience in a supportive and caring community. Each child came and sat in the big chair with me as they 'shared'. Children did as much as they wanted to do depending on their level of comfort. For some children, their initial contributions would have been limited to holding up an object. Then I talked about it with them. The rest of the children are always eager to ask questions and provide their own experiences and talk about the sharing topic. Sam also was assigned a 'sharing day'. In the early days he would bring a photograph and hold it up for the class to see. In later months he might share his special sight word books that had been prepared for him. The children would ask questions and make comments. Sometimes Sam would respond and other times not. But at the conclusion of his sharing time, the class would break into spontaneous cheering and applause. Over time Sam came to anticipate this reaction and smile broadly at their response.

In the days before the buddy program, the adults responsible for Sam's learning went to great lengths to create 'natural reinforcers' for on task and appropriate behaviors. Often it was a guessing game to come up with ideas to encourage Sam to keep working, to accomplish adult prepared jobs. There were often concerns about Sam's fine

Continued

muscle deveopment, and we consulted numerous experts about the best strategies to use. But as time went on we, the adults in the room, began to learn many things about children and friendships, and what really important learning could look like. When, as teachers, we were willing to step back and encourage other experts to do the teaching, everyone's learning experiences became richer and more relevant.

One morning during sharing and snack time, the camera caught a valuable learning moment that would not have occurred without the buddy program. All the children were huddled around the big chair while an excited classmate chatted about her weekend adventures. In the far back corner, disinterested in the story, my wiggly Leroy was off-task. If I had been a more attentive teacher, I would have noticed his unfocused behavior and reminded him of good audience skills. However, lost would have been a precious teaching moment. Linda Hof's (our video ethnographer) attention was diverted from the front of the group when Leroy whispered to her, 'You've got to see this.' After opening his 'Dunkeroo' package, Leroy had offered Sam a tiny cookie. He then showed Sam how to dip the cookie into the miniature container of chocolate icing. Sam did not need much instruction and was quick to pick up this new skill. Leroy was absolutely thrilled with the success of the lesson. They continued dipping and nibbling together until all the cookies were gone. Leroy then showed Sam how they could finish the sweet treat by dipping their fingers into the icing and licking them off. This experience, this learning would not have been accessible to Sam if he were working directly with an adult; in fact, this would have been seen as inappropriate and unsanitary behavior and halted immediately. But Sam was learning 'kid skills' – those important things that separate children from adults and make childhood such a special time. Sam and Leroy were being two little boys, sharing a common language with a wonderful, natural reinforcer!

One of the other components of our buddy program was regular Sign Language instruction for the class led by Pippi. Because of Sam's limited language we had been exploring alternate methods of communication, and he had been learning sign language since kindergarten. The children loved participating in this activity and they were quick learners. Soon they were comfortable signing all the letters of the alphabet and were beginning to communicate with each other. Pippi started to teach the signs that went with songs that the children were learning in music class, and they began performing them at assemblies.

Continued

Sam would stand proudly on stage always surrounded by his friends. The parent of one of my students was enrolled in a Seniors Support Care Worker Program at the community college, and he became interested in the children's eagerness to learn a new skill in order to communicate with Sam. He saw the benefits of a signing program for seniors who were unable to communicate their needs effectively. For his final project, he invited our class to be guest speakers at the college. This wonderful group of seven year olds performed their songs and spoke confidently about the importance of the buddy program. The adult students learned many things that day, inspired by these young children's dedication and caring of their special friend.

As the first year of the program neared an end, I felt great sadness in having to say goodbye to this wonderful group of children. I felt that the success of the program was the direct result of having such a sensitive and compassionate group of children to work with. I wanted our experience to go on forever. Not only were the children moving on to new classes, but a new elementary school was opening in our neighborhood and many of my students were changing schools. It was with heavy hearts that we said our goodbyes. On the last day of school, just before dismissal time, Sam's mother came into the classroom, wanting to speak to the children. She presented us with a special citizenship award for the kindness and caring that we had shown Sam. She stated that for the first time since her son had started school, she had felt like just another Mom dropping her son off at school; she know that he was happy with his friends, learning and growing and just being a kid.

This story describes an attempt to try a different path through the educational terrain with a group of children. This is the story of one classroom community who tried to create something different for themselves. It was an attempt to explore the relationships between people, over time, as they tried to build an inclusive and supportive educational environment in which all members had the opportunity to explore, learn and grow. Our learning community was made of a diverse group of participants; little mention has been made of the specific challenges and disabilities of the other children who came through my door, Sam's buddies. It is through Sam's story that I tried to identify how we learned to support each other. I realized that the essence of this project was the building of relationships in the classroom community. It was an opportunity for children and adults to

Continued

work together to support the needs of all classroom participants. Everyone worked together to create an honoured place within our classroom walls for Sam. This was not a program; there were no manuals, no rules or reminders, no student activity sheets. This is merely the story of one group of citizens who were trying to make a difference in their world, and one teacher, looking for the possibility of a different educational road.

This is as it must be. In the final analysis, it will always be the classroom teacher who has the power to lift the spirit of the individual child and beat the drums for the communal dance. (Paley, 1995: 114)

In a later discussion, Suzanne said:

I have tried to speak with my students about the future. They know that I am only walking along their road for a very short time, and I understand that their time in my classroom will become a distant hazy memory. As a teacher, I am able to leave just a little bit of myself with my students. But they will remain Sam's peers, his community and his future. It is within their power to make lasting changes, not only in the educational system but also to have a dynamic impact on how society chooses to look at its citizens. These children are the ones who have the voices to demand something different, something better. They can choose to maintain their position next to Sam, to cherish his friendship and to celebrate his successes. Sam is just one example of what inclusion can mean and these children are just one small group of citizens trying to make a difference. Will they choose to make that difference? I believe so. These children, Sam's friends, are powerful agents of change, and, knowing them, I certainly feel more hopeful for the future.

Students come into our lives and are HUGE. Then they go away. Over time, some of them come to represent something we were struggling with – some big question or insight or triumph or defeat. Their names are never forgotten and are carried with us always. Those of us who, after long days in the classroom, climb the hill to the university every Wednesday to meet together in our small, blue room around the oval table have brought Ashif and Tim and Jennifer and the many other children and teachers and families with us. Together we have come to know them better – living with them over time, watching and listening and exploring beneath the superficial, finding delight in the complexities that enrich all human beings. Their stories have become part of our lives and thus part of our individual classrooms. While in the classroom we teach that a proper story has a beginning, middle and end, we are able to accept that these stories do not have endings – just middles. When we try to articulate what it is that keeps us climbing the hill, the word we inevitably come up with is 'possibilities' – the possibility of understanding more, the possibility that things will change, the possibility of being able to create better opportunities for Jake and Rachel and Surjeet and the Grandmas to come. It is possibilities that keep us taking deep breaths and keep us directed towards the future.

Chapter 7
Being In-Between

Giving With Both Hands

Kathy Neilson

For me the act of teaching is a dilemma. I find myself teetering on a knife-edge between two irreconcilable tasks, tilting to one side for a while and then to the other. I attempt to offer my students encounters with new knowledge, skills, practices, values – the potential for an expanded world – but always within mandated and rigid schedules, codes for behavior and dress, required demonstrations of productivity – the markers of well socialized students. All term long I strive to provide opportunities for engaging with valued knowledge and cultural practices by means that will allow each student to incorporate those practices into their lived worlds in personally meaningful ways – and then at the end of the term I am required to assign each one to a place on an established, steeply graded hierarchy of identities. Teaching feels to me like giving with one hand while taking away with the other.

I realized at the end of my first term as a teacher that something was wrong – that almost everything I believed in about children and learning and that everything I was trying to achieve in my classroom was being violated in the act of writing report cards. What I really wanted my students to learn was an appreciation of culture, of the achievements and possibilities of human endeavor. I wanted to enable them to find their own voices and join in that great human conversation.

Doing report cards forced me to categorize the same students I was trying to free, to impose limitations on them when all term long I had

Continued

been trying to widen their scope of possibilities. This felt all wrong – I felt like I was being asked to violate a trust. None of my colleagues, however, seemed to be feeling this crisis.

I assumed the problem was in me. I began to doubt my own goals, to see them as naïve and idealistic. I was, after all, a child of the 60s; perhaps it was inevitable that my philosophy would be shaped by unrealistic and utopian notions. I spent a large portion of the next 20 years thinking about, talking about, struggling with many peda-gogical experiments, especially in methods of assessment and evalu-ation, trying to make my work congruent with a set of beliefs that I somehow could not quite shake.

In this chapter, we consider an issue that we think permeated our work in classrooms and in research. We have come to see that many of our research dilemmas were as a result of our positioning 'in-between'. Our teacher members interacted closely with groups of students every day, while at the same time being employed by, and owing allegiance to large bureaucracies (schools and the Ministry of Education). Our university-based members owed allegiance to their own research communities with their practices and standards of practice, and at the same time, were inter-acting with teacher researchers whose seemingly less tidy and less systematic work seemed nonetheless important and significant. Everyone belongs to multiple communities, of course, and the conventional practices, beliefs and positions of some of our communities are sometimes congruent with, but at other times, contradictory of others.

Aoki (2005) introduced the notion of teaching as 'indwelling' between curriculum-as-planned, and curriculum-as-lived experience, arguing that this is a necessary and beneficial place for teachers, as it both makes for sensitivity to ongoing situations but also for accountability to our wider societies. Kathy Neilson's story about teaching in secondary schools presents a different aspect – the deep discomfort – of the 'in-betweeness' of teaching. Many of the questions and issues raised in TARG can been seen as arising from the tension between the needs – physical, emotional, social, intellectual or moral – of individuals and the demands of a social system, in this case, *school* or *research*. The irreconcilability of these competing needs is at the heart of the difficulties and struggles that the participants described and that prompted their ventures into research.

Teacher TARG members were often critical of the system practices of school (and what school required of them as employees of bureaucracies).

They saw how these practices often conflicted with their conviction that sometimes, 'the rules' or 'the curriculum' just did not work in their classrooms or were detrimental to the education of the particular children with whom they worked. Novice and experienced teachers alike discovered that their discomfort and sometimes anger with some school practices were shared, and that many of these issues had been discussed in academic literature. Finding the vocabulary and allies to critique these practices was an unexpected boon of our work together. At the same time, teachers recognized that public schooling, as presently conceived, requires system-wide statements of goals, aims and objectives.

Not only the teachers felt that they had competing allegiances. Linda Hof's story of her video work for the research that underlay *Learning English at School* shows her struggle with this.

Video Ethnographer

My job, for more than 30 years, has been as the Television Resources person for the Faculty of Education at Simon Fraser University. I do everything from purchasing videos to producing them. But the work that is closest to my heart, however, is the ethnographic filming I do with teachers in their classrooms.

As an ethnographer in most research projects, I have had to be seen as neutral, a mere extension of the camera. My job is to reflect reality, not alter it. In cases where I don't like what I see, this allows me to hide behind the camera and the protocol – to justify my role in the classroom as only a technician and to avoid taking any responsibility for the scenes unfolding before me.

But it has become increasingly difficult for me to record classroom situations where there is dissonance between the teacher's intent and effect. For example, I spent three years following a group of six children from Kindergarten through Grade 2, documenting the impact of three different teaching styles on their school lives. Over the three years, they became 'MY' kids, and I had a difficult time watching a lot of what I saw.

I still wonder – as an adult in those classrooms, was I inadvertently condoning the teachers' behavior as I stood behind my camera? What was my personal responsibility to those children? Their faces filled my screen leaving me with the powerful video images I captured of

---

Continued

> children turning more and more inward – away from their rejection
> by teachers who wanted 'the right kind of students'. MY six clearly
> weren't the right kind. I'm not sure that I will ever be able to stand in
> a classroom and record research in that way again.

Linda brings up a somewhat different aspect of living in-between: she
lived in between the requirements of noninterventionist research and her
own ethical positions. She was critical of teacher practices in some cases,
but as a 'data-gatherer', she felt she could not voice her concerns. Kelleen
also became convinced through the work for *Learning English at School* that
the role of non-engaged observer was problematic in schools, and that
cooperation between teachers and university researchers might offer more
possibilities for real change in classrooms. This position was not, however,
without other difficulties, to be discussed later.

The TARG members' experience and Aoki's perception of 'dwelling in
the zone of between' are echoed in Habermas's (1996) concept of system
and lifeworld. '[S]ystem refers to the market economy and the state
apparatus. The lifeworld is the immediate milieu of the individual social
actor' (Soules, 2008). For Habermas, human experience is shaped by
the interplay of the individual's lifeworld and the social systems in which
s/he participates. Kincheloe (2003) argued that 'system' is increasingly
dominant in schools, noting that in a new world order that stresses technical knowledge and standards, there is increasingly heavy reliance on
experts who produce instrumental knowledge far away from the contexts
about which they profess. The resulting 'dumbing-down' of citizens,
parents, teachers and other persons who work is, he argued, one of the
ways in which there has been a centralization of power and 'scientific
management' of societies. He saw the production of increasingly specific
curricular outcomes in schools as part of this trend toward deskilling
professionals, and toward convincing them that outside experts can produce descriptions of 'best practices' that teachers need only replicate.
To counter such a trend, he argued that teacher research that confronts
questions like: 'What is the social role of schooling in a democratic society? ... What is the political impact of particular educational practices?'
(Kincheloe, 2003: 20), involves teachers in work that will democratically
reform education.

At bottom, the inquiries pursued by TARG teachers were fundamental
questions like those Kinchloe identified. All grew out of the tensions they
experienced as 'dwellers in between', caught between their own moral

imperatives to honour the individuality of each child in their classes and the expectations of state-mandated curriculum and school structures. It was the issues associated with individual child – or particular children – that initially raised questions about how to create equitable classrooms and practices or about how to continue to live in between these competing demands. Abu El-Haj described exactly the same concerns and approach in the Teachers Learning Co-operative:

> These processes allow educators to see where tensions lie between [a child's] individual strengths, standards and values and those of the teacher, classroom, or dominant structures of schooling. (El-Haj, 2003: 832)

For the university-based TARG members, the tensions they faced were between scientific research conventions and the important transformative research of their teacher colleagues. Realizing the importance of the knowledge the teachers were producing, and the enthusiastic reception it was receiving when TARG gave presentations, the university-based researchers were initially unsure about how to represent this knowledge collaboratively with the teachers. They knew the teacher research would not be accepted without considerable revision by academic journals, and they were initially unfamiliar with practitioner journals. They too felt caught between.

The Pivotal Role of Dialogue for Living In-Between ...

In TARG, conversations wove together research ideas, challenging questions and discussions of other classroom-based studies and classroom activities through video data or stories brought to the table each week. These conversations served several important functions. First, the regular renewing of shared values and visions for practice provided sustenance for coping with the daily stresses of living in between. Members rotated through the roles of providing or needing energy and support. The weekly restating of beliefs and perceptions strengthened both the sense of the legitimacy of those understandings and also the resolve to act upon them. A second function of the discourse was to provide language for resisting the dominant practices that seemed so problematic. Conversations like those of TARG or TLC enabled teachers (and researchers) to 'resist constructing children as successes or failures ... to consider the institutional structures that resist the child (Carini, 2001) and to imagine changing classroom practices to allow each child's meaningful participation in the community' (El-Haj, 2003: 841). A third function was the exchange of knowledge and expertise. Teacher members of TARG found it helpful to draw on the research expertise provided by Kelleen, Bonnie and Roumi – who, in turn, gained from the teachers' knowledge of daily practice.

Another Kind of In-Between

The coming together of teachers and academic researchers created another kind of in-between. TARG's inception generated a space between teaching and research where, once again, conversation was the catalyst for mutual growth. In a doctoral thesis that concerned the first year of the life of TARG, Bonnie Waterstone described our conversations as a curriculum designed to teach us how to do collaborative research, in ways that respected our differently situated perspectives. She characterized our dialog as 'rhizomatic':

> I use the metaphor of the rhizome (from Deleuze & Guattari, 1987) to describe [the] conversational flow in TARG. Mary Leach and Megan Boler (1998) claim this rhizomatic movement, growing 'underground, sideways; functioning as a relay, connecting, circulating, moving on', better expresses the multiple dimensionality of women's talk.

As we began to design research, we spent many weekly sessions trying 'to communicate expectations, to offer alternative wordings, and to extend each other's thinking in conceptualizing an inquiry' (Leach & Boler, 1998: 158). Bonnie also saw this as curricular work:

> Refining research foci through such a conversational curriculum differed from other ways we might have learned – such as reading and discussing written guidelines for how to design qualitative research questions ... There were practical consequences of this muddling around – we spent many sessions defining each research focus. But our more flexible way resonated with collaborative research values about joint ownership of the research process. It also resonated with an understanding that learning from experience, and having students experience expectations rather than just telling them the 'rules', is good pedagogical practice ... Our protracted grappling with research design was mediated by and represented our values/ beliefs about learning and about collaborative research.

Bonnie saw the time of research design as pivotal in TARG's first year partly because it was one of the times when our different positions in the educational hierarchy came up against our aspiration to maintain as equitable a collaboration as possible. She noted:

> In the rhizomatic movement of our conversations, our process of learning the genre of research was multi-dimensional: feedback came from all directions, and the person describing their research was responding to questions and concerns from everyone present. Granted, Kelleen's feedback had a great deal of power, especially for this particular activity of designing research. [Roumi] [another doctoral student member] and I, following Kelleen's model, often phrased our suggestions in tentative ways. The direction of our curriculum was negotiated within the conversations, with the university-based researchers' voices stronger – Kelleen's perhaps the strongest – but with a full component of teachers as well. Sometimes the teachers' comments to each other seemed more persuasive.

Members of TARG came to understand that they were not interested in homogenizing the worlds of university researchers and the worlds of teachers, as do some advocates of teacher research. Rather, they modeled themselves as a 'research group' somewhat like those in scientific research. Jacoby and Gonzalez (1991) described a physics laboratory research group in which they came to see the expertise in the group circulating. In the physics group's discussions, the tenured professor-leader of the lab sometimes saw himself and sometimes was seen as the most knowledgeable, but at other times, graduate student laboratory assistants (closer to actual lab events) had necessary knowledge. Jacoby and Gonzalez argue that 'viewing expert–novice as a bipolar dichotomy or as some set of relative statuses to which individuals may be assigned fails to capture both the complexity of what it means to "know things" and the dynamic fluidity of expert-novice relations as they are constituted in unfolding interaction' (Jacoby & Gonzalez, 1991: 152). This notion of fluidity in expertise was a founding normative principle of TARG, and was taken up in a variety of ways in our discussions. As aptly put by the educational philosopher, Alexander Sidorkin, we saw:

> Truth reveals when one can hear and comprehend both or all voices simultaneously, and more than that, when one's own voice joins in and creates something similar to a musical chord. In a chord, voices remain different, but they form a different type of music, which is in principle unattainable by a single voice. (Sidorkin, 1999: 30)

This metaphor represents a value consciously embraced by TARG: we were firmly of the opinion that much of the power of our work together was because we did not try to turn teachers into academic researchers, or academic researchers into teacher action researchers. Rather, we were content to let our various voices co-mingle.

However, the chords we made were not always harmonious. The ethics of research, and whether it was a form of surveillance which only benefited the researchers, was a topic on which TARG members did not agree. Nevertheless as the following examples suggest, we managed to maintain these different perspectives on this issue *and* continue to move our work forward. On one occasion when Joanne Thompson described her research with her buddy group, Corey Denos asked, 'Does the teacher want to see your transcriptions?' The conversation continued:

> **Corey:** I've never worked with a researcher before, but it seems to me that it would be such an opportunity [for the teacher] to be along with you examining them [the transcripts], rather than waiting to be questioned – did this go the way you thought it was going to go? Puts me [the teacher] on the spot. But if I was actively involved with you every day, looking at what the data was, then it's a learning experience.

> **Joanne:** To play the devil's advocate, though, if I showed them to you every day, then every day you would go away with some kind of interpretation and you would change what is naturally your behavior. And so, what I had envisioned, was that I would observe for a period of time, and then we would be able to sit down and conference about some things.

> **Corey:** I guess, personally, that feels threatening to me. It feels like you have more power than me because you are observing me privately inside yourself, and not letting me in on the same stuff. It feels threatening to me, so anything you would say would have an extra element, I would feel defensive.

This discussion of the difficulties with educational research, as it is usually done (by researchers with little or no collaboration with research 'subjects'), was a concern that did not go away for members of TARG.

Another particularly 'discordant' example occurred during a conversation when we began to plan this book. After an evening of discussion of an early draft that Corey had produced, two members reported back to the larger group that they had noticed that the majority of the stories we told about the children in our classes could be seen as representing the perspectives of white Anglo middle-class women teachers (although not all of us were white or Anglo or middle-class or teachers), and that it might be good in the book to address the fact that we did speak from this perspective – and that naturally, this perspective was limited. They also remarked that there was the danger that the stories could be exploitative of the children and their parents – that is, while the benefit for TARG members in telling these stories was obvious, the benefit for the children and their families might not be so obvious. Some of us agreed with these observations; others did not and felt that 'exploitation' was no part of their intentions in telling these stories, or in what these stories accomplished. Some of those who did not agree were upset and felt accused in a way that threatened their sense of themselves as caring teachers. Some of the teachers had shared their research with their students and their parents and felt that the stories represented children's and parents' voices as well as theirs. This conversation brought up many unresolved issues in our research, and in research generally, and like other researchers who have worried about such issues, we did not develop consensus on how they might be resolved. This discussion did, however, make us alert to the differences among us, and we seemed to become increasingly more comfortable subsequently with considering how our stories, convictions and beliefs might be formed as a result not only of our social positions (employment situations, color, ethnicity, gender, age and so on), but also as a result of our differing life experiences and personal circumstances. Clearly, our shared identity as dwellers in-between did not eliminate or override our other differences. This is, of course, an ongoing issue and we will continue to think critically about whose points of view are not represented in, and who benefited from our research in TARG, and in our schools and universities. In particular, Bonnie Waterstone's (2003) analysis of our first year together showed the complexities of a commitment to an ethic of inclusion: she argued that, ironically, this shared ethic may have silenced voices who saw matters differently. As she put it:

> Investigating TARG, I wondered how we as a group demonstrated in our own research collaboration the kinds of inclusion and participation we valued in the classroom (Waterstone, 2003). The tensions that lived in the in-between space we occupied, the place between teaching and research practices, with their different investments, interests, and needs seemed to become heightened at certain thresholds. One of these was when we first began to design research questions to guide classroom inquiries. Teachers in the group, new to formulating research questions, struggled to 'get it right' as it became clear that not just any research question would work in TARG. To 'fit' within TARG's parameters, a research question would have to be answerable by the research methods we would use – for example, audio- and videotapes

of classroom interactions – and be based on the sociocultural premise that learning occurs in social interactions. Like AA oldtimers selectively building on elements of newcomers' stories (Cain, 1991), those of us in TARG with more research experience disciplined and nurtured tentative research plans, reinforcing ideas that seemed promising, or spending successive weeks reframing others. At some of these stress points, our differential expertise threatened the valued co-ownership of TARG's agenda. We handled such tension through this method of giving friendly, but carefully critical, responses to each other's ideas.

As we have stated elsewhere, sometimes 'shared norms' can silence dissent. The conversations in TARG built in certain directions, and not others, based on how ideas or stories were taken up (or not). Some stories were received enthusiastically and guided discussion for a while; their topics (a particular child, a particular classroom dilemma) became familiar and recognizable over time. A story, DeCerteau (1984) says, 'authorizes' the creation of a field for action (DeCerteau, 1984: 125), sketches out 'habitable places' (DeCerteau, 1984: 106). As I suggested in my research on TARG's conversations, 'we easily inhabited some places. Other stories seemed to offer only temporary lodgings, or remained in shadow, unhabitable' (Waterstone, 2003: 93). One example of this is how I chose not to tell certain stories during the first year of TARG's existence (when the weekly conversations were forming the data for my doctoral work). I kept silent about being a lesbian. A few months later, I shared with the group the part of my dissertation that analyzed my silence in a particular conversation. In part, this analysis explained how I had not wanted to be disloyal to the norm I felt was assumed in TARG – that we were a group of heterosexual women. By opening this up, the ways we were inevitably and constantly in a process of including/excluding as we negotiated community, simply by choosing to follow up one topic and thus foreclosing another, became more visible. This renewed our commitment to recognizing and valuing diverse and dissenting stories, points of view, even ideas for what might count as research. Understanding community as 'the product of work, of struggle' (Martin & Mohanty, 1986: 210, quoted in Waterstone, 2003: 135), means that such dilemmas of exclusion/inclusion must always be confronted; to assume that exclusion is not happening is naive. Rather, it is a question of becoming more aware that genuine diversity must be constantly negotiated.

Conclusion

> Participatory action research groups and projects might be seen as open-textured networks established for communication and exploration of social problems or issues and as having relationships with other networks and organizations in which members also participate. (Kemmis & McTaggart, 2005: 584)

Denzin (2000) called for new paradigms of research to address the complex practices and politics of interpretation and inquiry, to not only describe situated worlds well but to remember that the stories we tell 'should articulate a politics of hope … [they] should criticize how things are and imagine how they could be different' (Denzin, 2000: 916). The stories told and analyzed in the collaborative conversations of TARG, the renewal/reiteration of shared understandings, values, and approaches supported TARG members in sustaining their commitment to larger issues of social justice through the in-between difficulties and challenges of teaching in schools. We discuss some of the benefits of TARG for its members in the next and final chapter.

Chapter 8
Conclusion

> *[Action researchers] regard their research practices as constructed*
> *and open to reconstruction. They do not regard the research process as*
> *the application of fixed and preformed research techniques to the*
> *particular 'applied' problem with which they are concerned. On the*
> *contrary, they regard their research practices as a matter of borrowing,*
> *constructing, and reconstructing research methods and techniques*
> *to throw light on the nature, processes, and consequences of*
> *the particular object they are studying ... transforming themselves*
> *as researchers, transforming their research practices, and transforming*
> *the practice settings of their research.*
> Kemmis and McTaggart, 2005: 575

In this book, we have presented some of the work done by teachers, graduate students, a videoethnographer and a professor, as they collaboratively
investigated educational questions of interest to them. Our diverse studies
were 'intertextual', in that they all had effects on one another, and in some
ways echoed one another. We used a variety of research techniques, means
of reporting and analyzing data. In this chapter, we conclude this book by
examining briefly what sort of resource TARG was for its members, and if
the transformation Kemmis and McTaggart spoke about was a result of
this work.

We have been careful to note that TARG resulted in *participant* development, not just *teacher* development. The teachers in TARG certainly
expressed changes in their thinking and practice that they attributed to
researching practice. As Suzanne Rowbotham put it recently, 'TARG helped
me to be curious. Now when something happens in a classroom, I ask a
thousand questions about it, not just how can I stop this, or encourage
this?' Colleen Tsoukalas said about educational research,

> I used to think it was something those university people did up there
> [SFU is on a mountain]. I guess if I were to approach it with my students,

when we do research, it's finding something that makes you go, 'Hmmm, I wonder what's going on here?' And going to all the resources you can find to satisfy your curiosity, whether that's writing done by other people, whether that's talking to people, whether it's going to the library, whatever that might be. It's trying to give you more answers to what you've sort of been curious about.

Colleen went on to say she read other people's research differently as a result of engaging in her own and by participating in TARG: that she was not intimidated anymore, and realized that research was 'not terribly technical'. (We interpret Colleen's meaning of 'technical' to imply students and teachers could not participate in it.)

The university-based TARG members also found the group's dialogue to have important effects on their own teaching, thinking and writing. In addition to all she had learned from TARG about classrooms and teachers' worlds, Kelleen spoke often about how participation in TARG had taught her to listen more attentively to her students, and to feel less need to try to control university classroom interactions or to solve all pedagogical problems students raised, realizing that even with experience and support, teachers were unable to solve all the problems they would encounter. She became interested in Mary Louise Pratt's (1999) discussions of classrooms as 'contact zones' in which everyone is aware that no single set of rules or norms are shared by participants, and the assumption of shared norms serves to silence 'others'. Pratt describes teaching in such contact zones:

> The lecturer's traditional (imagined) task – unifying the world in the class' eyes by means of a monologue that rings equally coherent, revealing, and true for all, forging an ad hoc community, homogeneous with respect to one's own words – this task became not only impossible but anomalous and unimaginable. Instead, one had to work in the knowledge that whatever one said was going to be systematically received in radically heterogeneous ways that we were neither able nor entitled to prescribe.

Pratt's discussion of classrooms in which difference in perspectives was expected and welcomed suggested potentially new ways for university classrooms to operate. The open discussions and debates and disagreements that occurred in TARG, the shifting expertise, and participants' chosen commitment to continue to work together, were illustrative of new ways of teaching that Kelleen appreciated very much. Immersed in doctoral work, Bonnie was first surprised by the power of the stories from the classroom to communicate ideas about community, identity, and schooling; in teaching, she learned to use stories to illustrate concepts and to bring the lives of children into the foreground. In researching and writing, Bonnie became intrigued by how narratives function in identity formation and community solidarity. Clearly, the university-based participants learned a great deal through our activities.

Kathy Neilson, an experienced teacher, who was situated in between the university and teachers in her work as a coordinator of a university-credentialed professional development program spoke of how TARG had been of benefit to her:

> My search for answers to the problem of being in-between brought me finally to the academy, where I discovered I was not alone in my concerns. As I embarked on a Masters degree, I encountered writers and theorists who echoed my perceptions and contextualized the issues in ways that affirmed and clarified my own intuitions. But no one offered any answers. Then I was invited to join TARG, where I found something better than answers: a caring, interested, thoughtful, funny group of women who absolutely understood my dilemma from the inside and who willingly listened and shared their own feelings and survival strategies ... those weekly meetings pulled me back from the brink of despair and gave me the courage to find my own answer – and to *finally* finish my thesis.

The 'curriculum' of TARG was aimed toward learning how to do and represent educational research and create knowledge from everyday activities. Engaging in sustained reflection on the stories of daily life in classrooms and grappling as a community of inquiry with dilemmas presented in these stories was a powerful tool for participant development.

Conclusion

This book had, as we said earlier, a modest aim: to describe and try to understand work that we have been engaged in as teachers and academics over the past five or so years in trying to understand how classrooms might be better for children of diverse abilities, backgrounds and socio-economic circumstances. The previous chapters outline some of what we have come to learn about school classrooms and difference. We offer them not as guides for what other teachers might do with students in their classrooms – we are sensitized to how 'help' can diminish one's sense of agency and responsibility. Rather, we hope these stories might encourage others to think deeply about their classrooms and the children for which they have responsibility. By going to new places with those children, it may be that all of our lives will be enriched. Perhaps an unexpected result of the work has been how TARG itself evolved into a community of learners that offered members an experience of what they wished to provide for their students. We end with Suzanne Rowbotham's description of her idea of community, which can be applied to classrooms as well as to TARG:

> When I envision community, I picture a flock of geese flying south on a crisp autumn day. They have come together with a goal, which is of utmost importance to them all, survival. In this group there are those that have made this journey before, experts in the task, and there are those that are young, inexperienced and making their first flight. Watching them fly overhead, I am unable to identify the competency of any particular bird; each does what it is capable of as it works towards the common goal.

Notes

1. In our third year, we were fortunate to have the participation for a time of a young man who was a student teacher working with another TARG member and experienced teacher, Susie Sandhu. Satnam Chohal was a valued participant but he was unable to continue in TARG with the demands of a new teaching job and a new baby. Hereinafter, we will refer to TARG participants as female, as all but Satnam were.
2. A longer version of this paper has previously been published in *Language Arts* 80 (6), July 2003. Copyright 2003 by the National Council of Teachers of English. Used with permission.
3. In Chapter 7, we think about some of TARG's practices as providing us a community in which participants could try on identities as knowers, experts, novices and so on.
4. We are grateful to the Vancouver Centre of Excellence for Research in Immigration and Integration in the Metropolis (RIIM) for a research grant in 1996 (reported in Toohey *et al.*, 1999) to begin the research reported in this paper. Earlier versions of the paper was presented at the TESL-Ontario Research Symposia in November 2001, and at the 2003 International Conference on Creativity and Imagination in Education, Moscow, Russian Federation.
5. This and the other names in this paper are pseudonyms chosen by the participants.

References

Aoki, T. (2005) Teaching as indwelling between two curriculum worlds. In W. Pinar and R. Irwin (eds) *Curriculum in a New Key*. London: Laurence Erlbaum Publishers.

Bakhtin, M.M. (1981) *The Dialogical Imagination: Four Essays by M.M. Bakhtin* (M.E. Holqust and C. Emerson, trans.). Austin: University of Texas Press.

Bakhtin, M.M. (1984) *Problems of Dostoevsky's Poetics*. Minneapolis, MN: University of Minnesota Press.

Barbules, N. (1997) Teaching and the tragic sense of education. In N. Barbules and D. Hansen (eds) *Teaching and Its Predicament*. Boulder, CO: Westview Press.

Bass, V., Anderson-Patton, V. and Allender, J. (2002) Self-study as a way of teaching and learning: A research collaborative re-analysis of self-study teaching portfolios. In J.J. Loughran and T. Russell (eds) *Improving Teacher Education Practices Through Self-Study*. London: Falmer Press.

Bigdeli, S. (2007) ESL anxiety in Iranian immigrant women. Unpublished doctoral thesis, Simon Fraser University.

Bodone, F. (ed.) (2005) *What Difference Does Research Make and for Whom?* New York: Peter Lang.

Bruner, J. (1978) The role of dialogue in language acquisition. In A. Sinclair, R.J. Jarvelle and W.J.M. Levelt (eds) *The Child's Conception of Language*. New York: Springer-Verlag.

Cain, C. (1991) Personal stories: Identity acquisition and self-understanding in Alcoholics Anonymous. *Ethos* 19 (2), 210–253.

Carini, P. (2001) *Starting Strong: A Different Look at Children, Schools and Standards*. New York: Teachers College Record.

Carugati, F. (1999) From Piaget and Vygotsky to learning activities: A long journey and an inescapable issue. In M. Hedegaard and J. Lompscher (eds) *Learning Activity and Development* (pp. 235–248). Aarhus: Aarhus University Press.

Chu, C. (1999) Immigrant children mediators: Bridging the literacy gap in immigrant communities. *The New Review of Children's Literature and Librarianship* 5, 85–94.

Clandinin, D.J. and Connolly, M. (2000) *Narrative Inquiry, Experience and Story in Qualitative Research*. San Francisco: Jossey-Bass.

Cochran-Smith, M. and Lytle, S. (1999) The teacher research movement: A decade later. *Educational Researcher* 8 (7), 15–25.

Day, E. (2002) *Identity and the Young Language Learner: An Ethnographic Case Study*. Clevedon: Multilingual Matters.

DeCerteau, M. (1984) *The Practice of Everyday Life* (S. Rendall, trans.). Berkeley: University of California Press.

Deleuze, G. and Guattari, F. (1987) *A Thousand Plateaus: Capitalism and Schizophrenia*. Minneapolis, MN: University of Minnesota Press.

Denos, C. (2003) Negotiating for positions of power in a primary classroom. *Language Arts* 80 (6).

Denzin, N. (2000) The practices and politics of interpretation. In N. Denzin and Y. Lincoln (eds) *Handbook of Qualitative Research* (2nd edn) (pp. 897–922). Thousand Oaks, CA: Sage.

Dewey, J. (1916) *Democracy and Education*. New York: The Free Press.

El-Haj, T.R.A. (2003) Practicing for equity from the standpoint of the particular: Exploring the work of one urban teacher network. *Teachers College Record* 105 (5), 817–845.

Escobar, A. (1992) Culture, practice and politics: Anthropology and the study of social movements. *Critique of Anthropology* 12, 395–432.

Fals Borda, O. and Rahman, M. (1991) *Action and Knowledge: Breaking the Monopoly with Participatory Action Research*. New York: Apex Press.

Fishman, S. and McCarthy, L. (2000) *Unplayed Tapes: A Personal History of Collaborative Teacher Research*. New York: Teachers College Press.

Freebody, P. (2003) *Qualitative Research in Education: Interaction and Practice*. London: Sage Publications.

Freire, P. (1982) Creating alternative research methods: Learning to do it by doing it. In B. Hall, A. Gillette and R. Tandon (eds) *Creating Knowledge: A Monopoly?* New Delhi: Society for Participatory Research in Asia. Reprinted in Kemmis, L. and McTaggart, R. (eds) (1988) *The Action Research Reader*. Geelong, Australia: Deakin University Press.

Freire, P. (1998) *Pedagogy of Freedom: Ethics, Democracy and Civic Courage*. Boulder: Rowman and Littlefield.

Greene, M. (1988) *The Dialectic of Freedom*. New York: Teachers College Press.

Habermas, J. (1989) *The Structural Transformation of the Public Sphere: An Inquiry into a Category of Bourgeois Society* (T. Burger with the assistance of F. Lawrence, trans.). Cambridge, MA: MIT Press.

Habermas, J. (1996) *Between Facts and Norms* (W. Rehg, trans.). Cambridge, MA: MIT Press.

Holland, D., Skinner, D., Lachicotte, W. and Cain, C. (1998) *Identity and Agency in Cultural Worlds*. Cambridge, MA: Harvard University Press.

Jacoby, S. and Gonzalez, P. (1991) The constitution of expert-novice in scientific discourse. *Issues in Applied Linguistics* 2 (2), 149–181.

Jervis, K., Carr, E., Lockhart, P. and Rogers, J. (1996) Multiple entries to teacher inquiry: Dissolving boundaries between research and teaching. In L. Baker, P. Afflerbach and D. Reinking (eds) *Developing Engaged Readers in School and Home Communities* (pp. 247–268). Mahwah, NJ: Lawrence Erlbaum Associates.

Kemmis, S. and McTaggart, R. (2005) Participatory action research: Communicative action and the public sphere. In N. Denzin and Y. Lincoln (eds) *The Sage Handbook of Qualitative Research* (3rd edn). Thousand Oaks: Sage Publications.

Kincheloe, J. (2003) *Teachers as Researchers: Qualitative Inquiry as a Path to Empowerment* (2nd ed). London: RoutledgeFalmer.

Ladson-Billings, G. (1994) *The Dream Keepers: Successful Teachers of African American Children*. San Francisco, CA: Jossey-Bass.

Ladson-Billings, G. (2001) *Crossing Over to Canaan: The Journey of New Teachers in Diverse Classrooms*. San Francisco: Jossey-Bass Inc.

Lather, P. (1991) *Getting Smart: Research and Pedagogy Within the Postmodern*. New York: Routledge.

Lave, J. and Wenger, E. (1991) *Situated Learning: Legitimate Peripheral Participation.* Cambridge: Cambridge University Press.

Leach, M. and Boler, M. (1998) Gilles Deleuze: Practising education through flight and gossip. In M. Peters (ed.) *Naming the Multiple: Poststructuralism and Education* (pp. 149–172). Wesport, CN: Bergin & Garvey.

LeCompte, M.D. (1980) The civilizing of children: How young children learn to become students. *Journal of Thought* 15, 105–127.

Luke, A. (2004) Teaching after the market: From commodity to cosmopolitan. *Teachers College Record* 106 (7), 1422–1443.

McDermott, R. (1993) The acquisition of a child by a learning disability. In S. Chaiklin and J. Lave (eds) *Understanding Practice: Perspectives on Activity and Context.* Cambridge: Cambridge University Press.

Michaels, S. (2005) Can the intellectual affordances of working-class storytelling be leveraged in school? *Human Development* 48, 136–145.

Miller, L. (2005) Far from Narnia. *The New Yorker.* On WWW at http://www.newyorker.com/archive/2005/12/26/051226fa_fact. Accessed 31.10.07.

Mowat, F. (1996) *Owls in the Family.* New York, NY: Bell Doubleday Dell Pub.

Nolen, A. and Vander Putten, J. (2007) Action research in education: Addressing gaps in ethical principles and practices. *Educational Researcher* 36 (7), 401–407.

Norton, B. (2000) *Identity and Language Learning: Gender, Ethnicity and Educational Change.* Harlow: Longman/Pearson Education.

Nunan, D. (1992) *Collaborative Language Learning and Teaching.* Cambridge: Cambridge University Press.

Orellana, M.F. and Reynolds, J. (2008) Cultural modeling: Leveraging bilingual skills for school paraphrasing tasks. *Reading Research Quarterly* 13 (1), 50–65.

Paley, V.G. (1993) *You Can't Say You Can't Play.* Cambridge, MA: Harvard University Press.

Paley, V.G. (1995) *Kwanzaa and Me: A Teacher's Story.* Cambridge, MA: Harvard University Press.

Pappas, C. (1997) Making 'collaboration' problematic in collaborative school-university research: Studying with urban teacher researchers to transform literacy curriculum genres. In J. Flood, S.B. Heath and D. Lapp (eds) *Handbook of Research on Teaching Literacy Through the Communicative and Visual Arts* (pp. 215–231). London: Macmillan.

Pratt, M.L. (1999) Arts of the contact zone. In D. Bartholomae and A. Petroksky (eds) *Ways of Reading* (5th edn). New York: Bedford/St. Martin's.

Radnor, H. (2002) *Researching Your Professional Practice: Doing Interpretive Research.* Buckingham; Phildelphia, PA: Open University.

Rogoff, B. (1990) *Apprenticeship in Thinking: Cognitive Development in Social Context.* New York: Oxford University Press.

Rogoff, B. (1995) Observing sociocultural activity on three planes: Participatory appropriation, guided participation, and apprenticeship. In J. Wertsch, P. del Rio and A. Alvarez (eds) *Sociocultural Studies of Mind* (pp. 139–164). New York: Cambridge University Press.

Rogoff, B. (2003) *The Cultural Nature of Human Development.* Oxford: Oxford University Press.

Rogoff, B., Mosier, C., Mistry, J. and Goncü, A. (1993) Toddler's guided participation with their caregivers in cultural activity. In E.A. Forman, N. Minick and C.A. Stone (eds) *Contexts for Learning: Sociocultural Dynamics in Children's Development* (pp. 230–253). New York: Oxford University Press.

Rogoff, B., Goodman Turkanis, C. and Bartlett, L. (eds) (2001) *Learning Together: Children and Adults in a School Community*. Oxford: Oxford University Press.

Rowbotham, S. (2003) Sharing Sam's journey: The integration of one child with special needs. Unpublished Master's thesis, Simon Fraser University.

Rutherford, P. (2000) *Endless Propaganda: The Advertising of Public Goods*. Toronto: University of Toronto Press.

Samaras, A. and Freese, A. (2006) *Self-Study of Teaching Practices Primer*. New York: Peter Lang.

Shaw, C. (1947) *It Looked Like Spilt Milk*. New York: Harper Trophy.

Shields, C. (2002) *Unless: A Novel*. New York: Fourth Estate.

Sidorkin, A. (1999) *Beyond Discourse: Education, the Self and Dialogue*. Buffalo, NY: SUNY Press.

Siegel, B. (2003) *Helping Children with Autism Learn*. Oxford: Oxford University Press.

Soules, M. (2008) Jürgen Habermas and the Public Sphere. On WWW at www. mala.bc.ca/~soules/media301/habermas.htm. Accessed 21.1.08.

Taylor, C. (1989) *Sources of the Self: The Making of Modern Identity*. Cambridge MA: Harvard University Press.

Thompson, J. (2002) Effects of the buddy relationship on English language learners: An ethnographic case study. Unpublished Master's thesis, Simon Fraser University.

Toohey, K. (1999) SSHRC Standard Research Grant proposal.

Toohey, K. (2000) *Learning English at School: Identity, Social Relations and Classroom Practice*. Clevedon: Multilingual Matters.

Toohey, K. and Gajdamaschko, N. (2003) Communities of practice and learning initiative. Presentation at the *2003 International Conference on Creativity and Imagination in Education*. Moscow, Russian Federation.

Toohey, K., Waterstone, B. and Julé, A. (1999) Community of learners, carnival and participation in a Punjabi Sikh classroom. *The Canadian Modern Language Review* 56, 423–438.

Tse, L. (1996) Who decides? The effects of language brokering on home-school communication. *The Journal of Educational Issues of Language Minority Students* 16, 225–233.

Valdés, G. (2002) *Learning and Not Learning English: Latino Students in American Schools*. New York: NY: Teachers College Press.

Van der Klift, E. and Kunc, N. (1994) Hell-bent on helping: Benevolence, friendship and the politics of help. In J. Thousand, R. Villa and A. Nevin (eds) *Creativity and Collaborative Learning: A Practical Guide to Empowering Students and Teachers*. Baltimore: Paul Brookes.

Varenne, H. and McDermott, R. (1999) *Successful Failure: The School America Builds*. Boulder, CO: Westview Press.

Vygotsky, L.S. (1978) *Mind in Society: The Development of Higher Psychological Processes*. Cambridge, MA: Harvard University Press.

Wadsworth, Y. (1998) What is participatory action research? *Action Research International*. On WWW at http://www.scu.edu.au/schools/gcm/ar/ari/p-ywadsworth98.html. Accessed 21.1.08.

Walkerdine, V. (1998) *Counting Girls Out: Girls and Mathematics*. London: Falmer Press.

Waller, W. (1961) *The Sociology of Teaching*. New York: Russell and Russell.

Waterstone, B. (2003) Self, genre, community: Negotiating the landscape of a teacher/researcher collaboration. Unpublished doctoral dissertation, Simon Fraser University.

Weedon, C. (1987) *Feminist Practice and Poststructuralist Theory*. Oxford: Blackwell.

Wilcox, S., Watson, J. and Paterson, M. (2004) Self-study in professional practice. In J.J. Loughran, M.L. Hamilton, V.K. LaBoskey and T. Russell (eds) *International Handbook of Self-Study of Teaching and Teacher Education Practices* (Vol. 1). Dordrecht: Kluwer Academic Publishers.

Zeichner, K.M. and Noffke, S.E. (2001) Practitioner research. In V. Richardson (ed.) *Handbook of Research on Teaching* (4th edn). Washington, DC: American Educational Research Association.

For Product Safety Concerns and Information please contact our EU Authorised Representative:

Easy Access System Europe

Mustamäe tee 50

10621 Tallinn

Estonia

gpsr.requests@easproject.com

www.ingramcontent.com/pod-product-compliance
Lightning Source LLC
Chambersburg PA
CBHW062041270326
41929CB00014B/2491